Working women: opposing viewpoints

Working Women

Other Books of Related Interest:

Opposing Viewpoints Series

Family

Feminism

Male/Female Roles

"Congress shall make no law . . . abridging the freedom of speech, or of the press."

First Amendment to the U.S. Constitution

The basic foundation of our democracy is the First Amendment guarantee of freedom of expression. The Opposing Viewpoints series is dedicated to the concept of this basic freedom and the idea that it is more important to practice it than to enshrine it.

OPPOSING VIEWPOINTS® SERIES

Working Women

Christina Fisanick, Book Editor

GREENHAVEN PRESS
An imprint of Thomson Gale, a part of The Thomson Corporation

THOMSON
™
GALE

Detroit • New York • San Francisco • New Haven, Conn. • Waterville, Maine • London

Christine Nasso, *Publisher*
Elizabeth Des Chenes, *Managing Editor*

© 2008 The Gale Group.

Star logo is a trademark and Gale and Greenhaven Press are registered trademarks used herein under license.

For more information, contact:
Greenhaven Press
27500 Drake Rd.
Farmington Hills, MI 48331-3535
Or you can visit our Internet site at http://www.gale.com

Articles in Greenhaven Press anthologies are often edited for length to meet page require-ments. In addition, original titles of these works are changed to clearly present the main thesis and to explicitly indicate the author's opinion. Every effort is made to ensure that Greenhaven Press accurately reflects the original intent of the authors. Every effort has been made to trace the owners of copyrighted material.

Cover photograph reproduced by permission of photos.com.

LIBRARY OF CONGRESS CATALOGING-IN-PUBLICATION DATA

Working women / Christina Fisanick, book editor.
    p. cm. -- Opposing Viewpoints
  Includes bibliographical references and index.
  ISBN-13: 978-0-7377-3771-4 (hardcover)
  ISBN-13: 978-0-7377-3772-1 (pbk.)
  1. Working mothers--United States. 2. Sex discrimination in employment--United States. 3. Women employees--United States--Family relationships. 4. Social policy --United States. 5. Work and family--United States. I. Fisanick, Christina.
  HQ759.48.W675 2008
  331.40973--dc22

                                                                    2007030796

ISBN-10: 0-7377-3771-9
ISBN-10: 0-7377-3772-7

Printed in the United States of America
10 9 8 7 6 5 4 3 2 1

Contents

Chapter 3: What Can Be Done To Help Working Women Balance Work and Family Life?

Chapter 4: Are Working Women Good for Families?

Why Consider Opposing Viewpoints?

> *"The only way in which a human being can make some approach to knowing the whole of a subject is by hearing what can be said about it by persons of every variety of opinion and studying all modes in which it can be looked at by every character of mind. No wise man ever acquired his wisdom in any mode but this."*
>
> *John Stuart Mill*

In our media-intensive culture it is not difficult to find differing opinions. Thousands of newspapers and magazines and dozens of radio and television talk shows resound with differing points of view. The difficulty lies in deciding which opinion to agree with and which "experts" seem the most credible. The more inundated we become with differing opinions and claims, the more essential it is to hone critical reading and thinking skills to evaluate these ideas. Opposing Viewpoints books address this problem directly by presenting stimulating debates that can be used to enhance and teach these skills. The varied opinions contained in each book examine many different aspects of a single issue. While examining these conveniently edited opposing views, readers can develop critical thinking skills such as the ability to compare and contrast authors' credibility, facts, argumentation styles, use of persuasive techniques, and other stylistic tools. In short, the Opposing Viewpoints series is an ideal way to attain the higher-level thinking and reading skills so essential in a culture of diverse and contradictory opinions.

In addition to providing a tool for critical thinking, Opposing Viewpoints books challenge readers to question their own strongly held opinions and assumptions. Most people form their opinions on the basis of upbringing, peer pressure, and personal, cultural, or professional bias. By reading carefully balanced opposing views, readers must directly confront new ideas as well as the opinions of those with whom they disagree. This is not to simplistically argue that everyone who reads opposing views will—or should—change his or her opinion. Instead, the series enhances readers' understanding of their own views by encouraging confrontation with opposing ideas. Careful examination of others' views can lead to the readers' understanding of the logical inconsistencies in their own opinions, perspective on why they hold an opinion, and the consideration of the possibility that their opinion requires further evaluation.

Evaluating Other Opinions

To ensure that this type of examination occurs, Opposing Viewpoints books present all types of opinions. Prominent spokespeople on different sides of each issue as well as well-known professionals from many disciplines challenge the reader. An additional goal of the series is to provide a forum for other, less-known, or even unpopular viewpoints. The opinion of an ordinary person who has had to make the decision to cut off life support from a terminally ill relative, for example, may be just as valuable and provide just as much insight as a medical ethicist's professional opinion. The editors have two additional purposes in including these less-known views. One, the editors encourage readers to respect others' opinions—even when not enhanced by professional credibility. It is only by reading or listening to and objectively evaluating others' ideas that one can determine whether they are worthy of consideration. Two, the inclusion of such viewpoints encourages the important critical thinking skill of objectively evaluating an author's credentials and bias. This evaluation will illuminate an author's reasons for taking a particular stance on an issue and will aid in readers' evaluation of the author's ideas.

It is our hope that these books will give readers a deeper understanding of the issues debated and an appreciation of the complexity of even seemingly simple issues when good and honest people disagree. This awareness is particularly important in a democratic society such as ours in which people enter into public debate to determine the common good. Those with whom one disagrees should not be regarded as enemies but rather as people whose views deserve careful examination and may shed light on one's own.

Thomas Jefferson once said that "difference of opinion leads to inquiry, and inquiry to truth." Jefferson, a broadly educated man, argued that "if a nation expects to be ignorant and free . . . it expects what never was and never will be." As individuals and as a nation, it is imperative that we consider the opinions of others and examine them with skill and discernment. The Opposing Viewpoints series is intended to help readers achieve this goal.

David L. Bender and Bruno Leone,
Founders

Introduction

> *"Working moms dismiss nonworking moms as having nothing better to do than drive around in their Dodge Caravans listening to Barney tapes, while nonworking moms peg working moms as too caught up in their careers to care about their kids."*
>
> *Vera Gibbons,*
> *"The Mommy Wars"*

Since *Child* magazine coined the phrase in the 1980s, the Mommy Wars have been a regular feature of popular media. It seems that every media outlet from talk shows to blogs to nightly newscasts is eager to pit stay-at-home mothers against working mothers. Even women who have yet to have children or those women who may choose never to have them are caught up in this enduring debate because it gets at the very core of what society thinks of women and of their roles in the formation of the next generation. Regrettably, these public skirmishes have led to divisiveness among women who could be working together to make the world a better place.

Although the roots of the Mommy Wars stretch back to the 1960s when women began entering the workforce in greater numbers than ever before, the debate became visible to all Americans in the 1980s when the dialogue about mothering and motherhood came to the forefront of the public consciousness. In the early 2000s, the battle rages on, heating up every now and then as a new study or editorial points to further proof that one type of mother is better than the other. As more mothers become aware of this conflict, tensions arise between them at preschool, on the playground, and on the soccer field. In the end, these conflicts might be a response to guilt and defensiveness that women feel about their parenting choices. Leslie Morgan Steiner speaks of this in her book, *Mommy Wars: Stay-at-Home and Career Moms Face Off on Their Choices, Their Lives, Their Families*: "Motherhood in America is fraught with defensiveness, infighting, ignorance and judgment about what's best for kids, family, and women."

Some people argue that stay-at-home mothers are better for children. They assert that nothing is better for the growth and development of tomorrow's leaders than to have a mom that is available around the clock. They believe that mothers who work do so not out of necessity but because they are selfish and too career-focused. According to a 2001 study by the Joseph Rowntree Foundation, children whose mothers go back to work full-time demonstrate reduced academic achievement and psychological problems as adults. Taryn Zier wanted to avoid such potential after-effects, which is part of the reason why she decided to quit her job as a children's theater worker and stay home with her two children. Two months later, she didn't regret her decision: "Even though there have been hard days . . . I know I made the right decision. When I told people I was going to quit and stay home with my kids, the resounding response I received was that I would not regret it. And I am happy to say they [were] right."

On the other hand, some people argue that the danger of being a stay-at-home mom is that a woman may lack the financial independence either to leave a bad marriage or to support her family if her husband loses his job. They also think that children raised by working mothers are just as smart, well-behaved, and well-socialized as children raised by stay-at-home mothers. In fact, a study that appeared in the 1999 issue of *Developmental Psychology* concluded that children raised by working mothers were no different developmentally than children raised by stay-at-home mothers. Magazine editor Deborah Skolnick echoes this sentiment: "I think my kids are as well-behaved and as well-socialized, if not better, than a fair number of at-home moms."

Others argue that the Mommy Wars were started by the media and continue because the media have chosen to blow the issue way out of proportion. In fact, Kim Gandy, in 2007 the president of the National Organization of Women (NOW), asserts: "The most recent clash between stay-at-home moms and employed moms is a media-manufactured 'battle' that obscures the very real issues all moms and caregivers face." Jennifer Pozner also argues that the media plays a bigger role in the continuation of this war than most people realize and that most media outlets have another agenda in mind in continuously reigniting the Mommy Wars. After all, she says in *For Love or Money? Economics Takes a Backseat in Network Reports about Working Mothers*: "Media never question why fathers want careers, and rarely if ever imply that their presence in the workplace is bad for their children."

Ultimately, it seems that the Mommy Wars will never have a victor. There is plenty of scientific evidence to support the benefits and harm of both options. However, most parents are looking forward to a day when they do not have to choose between staying at home or going to work. As businesses develop more family-friendly policies and society learns to accept that fathers are equally effective at childrearing, the division between work and home will continue to shrink. As Cathy Young writes in *The Mommy Wars*: "In a generation or two, most people may find the polarization between 'working moms' and 'stay-at-home moms' [to be] meaningless." In the following chapters, the authors in *Opposing Viewpoints: Working Women* weigh in on the question of working moms and many more issues that affect working women: How Should Working Women Better Manage Their Finances? Are Working Women Discriminated Against in the Workplace? What Can Be Done to Help Working Women Balance Work and Family Life? Are Working Women Good for Families? While it is too soon to say if Young's prediction is right, it is certain that these debates will persist as long as women continue to enter the workplace.

OPPOSING
VIEWPOINTS®
SERIES

CHAPTER 1

How Should Working Women Better Manage Their Finances?

Chapter Preface

Between the 1980s and the early 2000s, rising awareness about the need for women to get more involved in managing their finances has led to an increasing number of publications that focus on the issues of gender in money matters. Sales of books marketed to women by popular financial wizards such as Suze Orman and Jean Chatzky are consistently high, and many financial magazines regularly feature columns and articles aimed at working women. Recently, as of 2007, the tax code has come under scrutiny. While some analysts argue that it is unfair to working women, other analysts disagree.

Given that the current tax laws were put into place during the 1930s through the 1950s, when fewer women were in the workforce, some critics have suggested that the laws do not adequately serve the needs of working women in the 2000s. According to Edward McCaffrey, researcher at the National Center for Policy Analysis, U.S. tax laws treat women workers unfairly and send them mixed messages about their value to the economy. In his 2002 report, he argues that working women, especially working married women, are penalized no matter into which tax bracket they fall. Married middle-income women are hit hard because they are taxed more heavily, and married low-income women are negatively affected because they lose the Earned Income Tax Credit. In the end, he states that married women are given conflicting messages about entering the workforce: "If you are middle- to upper-income and married, the incentive is not to work. If you are low-income and working, the incentive is not to marry."

By contrast, many experts may agree that when spouses earn salaries that are similar, then there is a penalty. Beyond that, however, the tax code is beneficial to married women. In an article on *MSN Money*, Liz Pulliam Weston debunks the myth that the tax code is biased against women. She states, "The reality is that even before the new tax act, more couples got a tax bonus when they married than suffered a penalty." She points to the statistics collected by the Congressional Budget Office in 1996. They showed that 51% of married couples received on average a $1,300 tax bonus just for being married.

In any case, whether tax laws are biased against women or not, more women must be involved in managing their own finances. As the women of the Baby Boom generation are beginning to find out, it is never too late or too early for women to understand where their money is going. The authors in this chapter make this argument clearly as they attempt to engage women in the current debates that affect working women and the money they make.

"*Most working women say that finance is the last thing on their minds after a gruelling day juggling work and domestic chores.*"

Women Must Take Charge of Their Finances

Udayan Ray and Archana Rai

In the following viewpoint, Udayan Ray and Archana Rai discuss the problems facing women who do not plan their finances carefully. It is important, they argue, for women to save and invest money and to be directly involved in their finances. Because women typically live longer than men, planning carefully for retirement is essential for economic well-being in later years. Ray and Rai are freelance writers for OutlookMoney, *an Indian personal finance magazine in which this excerpt appeared.*

As you read, consider the following questions:

1. What are four financial risks that women face?
2. What are the consequences of women being risk-averse?
3. In urban India, how much longer do women live than men?

"I should be taking more interest in the family's finances, but I don't," says Rita Kapur, 62, a retired academic. Her husband J. K. Kapur, also a retired academic, managed her finances through the three decades or so of her working life and the two years of retirement.

And this is the story across the country. Most working women say that finance is the last thing on their minds after a gruelling day juggling work and domestic chores. Others say that numbers only confuse them. And, of course, there are those who have been brought up to rely solely on male family members when it comes to managing money.

Which is why, in most families, men make the investment and long-term financial decisions. And this means that more often than not, the family's financial plan overlooks women-specific needs. Says Veer Sardesai, a wealth management expert, "Being proactive in managing money is a must for women, as it fosters personal empowerment. After all, women are the pivot of a family's wealth creation."

While working women substantially supplement the family income, homemakers make invaluable, but non-monetised, contributions, such as a plethora of domestic chores for which the family would have had to otherwise pay. As Vivek Kanwar, head, private banking, ICICI Bank, says: "Whether or not a woman has her own income, she needs to know how her family's money is invested."

While you may agree with Kanwar, you may wonder what "women-specific" financial needs are, and why family finances need to take them into account. Says Kartik Jhaveri, certified financial planner: "Typically, women face four primary risks—financial dependence, being given a lower share of family assets, failure of marriage, or an unequal division of inheritance." We take a look here at the major categories of situations that specifically impact women, and find out how they have a bearing on the family's finances.

Income Disruptions

"Given the fact that women experience greater disruption in earnings as they take career breaks to raise children and accommodate family contingencies, they need to have a holistic financial plan from a very early age," says Jhaveri.

Marriage and after. The first disruption in earnings is generally due to relocation after marriage, when the woman leaves her city or country. This, in many cases, forces her to take a break in her career.

Often, she is forced to settle for a lower-paying job (and a lower designation) in the new location. Then, there's the disruption in earning when a child is born. Many women take a break from their careers to tend to their offspring. If they decide to re-enter the workforce after a gap of a few years, they invariably have to compromise on designation and salary.

In some cases, there is another break where women give up work or take up lower-paying part-time or flexi-time jobs to provide care to elders at home. All these disruptions mean that though a woman and a man may have started their careers at the same time, she ends up earning far less when they both retire.

The effect of disruptions. If they've taken a break because of marriage or childbirth, women may be so busy billing and cooing that the thought of re-entering the workforce at a lower level does not bother them.

In the short term, they may not even notice that they are losing out in financial terms. However, in the long term, such disruptions hurt the family's wealth creation. Also, studies across the globe show that periodic income disruptions make women risk-averse. This means that they invest in lower-risk and fixed-income investment options such as fixed deposits and bonds for fear of losing money due to factors such as stock market fluctuations.

This, in turn, means that the growth in the value of investments doesn't beat inflation. As a result, in the long run, the purchasing power from accumulated wealth is far less than an investment mix that contains growth assets such as stocks, equity mutual funds and real estate—investments that beat inflation.

The outcome of the preference for fixed-income assets is obvious. The woman's savings will not suffice in her old age, and she'll have to depend on the retirement funds of her husband, or other sources.

The reality of divorce. This has got to be the worst of income disruptions for women, especially for homemakers who are solely dependent on their husbands for money. As per the law in India, women still can't hope for more than one-fifth of the husband's pre-tax income as alimony.

Dependant children complicate matters and can stretch finances to [the] breaking point. Therefore, though they may be blissfully happy together, it is important that couples don't lose sight of this unpleasant fact. Ideally, all money matters should be discussed by couples, investments made jointly and their details known to both partners.

Begin early. The ill-effects of income disruptions can be cushioned if women start taking interest in managing their finances early on. That's what Mumbai-based banker Lakshmi Vijayraman, 24, single and an only child, has done. She invested half of her first salary in a six-year RBI bond, ensuring that its maturity would coincide with her father's retirement.

She keeps her monthly expenses below Rs [Rupees, the currency in India] 9,000; with a monthly salary of Rs 20,000, she ensures that she has enough to save and invest for her future. As soon as she receives her pay cheque, she shifts almost half her salary to a joint account with her mother. "This ensures disciplined spending," says Vijayraman.

After having accumulated a sizeable sum in the joint account, she invested Rs 50,000 in mutual funds three months ago. For the past three years, she has been saving Rs 1,000 per month in a recurring deposit that will mature this October. "I began saving in the RD three years ago so that I can have a tidy sum for my wedding," she says.

Vijayraman has also invested in a monthly scheme with a jeweller to get some good deals in jewellery. "Although my father has saved enough, I feel equally responsible to contribute to my wedding," she says. And, of course, as a banker, she knows the importance of tax savings. She invests regularly in equity-linked saving schemes and National Savings Certificates.

Managing the disruptions. For women, among the shorter-term benefits of starting financial planning early is that upon marriage, they can share financial decision making with their husbands. Further, having created a cushion of accumulations, it is easier for them to make decisions involving the work-home balance, whether it is post-marriage or after childbirth. For instance, you need not get back to work for money when you actually want to stay home and bring up the baby. No, it's not easy. But as Rachna Bansal, 31, shows, it can be done.

Bansal, then a Delhi-based corporate trainer, married Vivek Abrol, a Dehradun-based hospitality entrepreneur some 18 months ago, and decided to relocate to Dehradun. This meant that she had to give up her full-time job. But, says Bansal: "The gap from work gave me time to think. I realised that flexi-time work is what suited me, since we were very keen to start a family soon after the marriage."

Bansal joined a training company on a flexi-time basis, but it meant that she had to be content with a lower income. She is now expecting her first child, which will mean one more disruption in her working life. But she has been through it once, and is prepared for it. "It was scary to leave a secure job and take this route. But now it feels all right. The intangibles are worth the scale-back in career," she says.

Being organised pays. Meaningful financial planning can help women in other ways too. Mumbai-based Roopa H. Sadani, a former team leader (HR), JP Morgan Chase, shows how. Sadani, 30, gave up her job almost a year ago when she was expecting her child.

Before that, she and her husband shared the financial burden of the household; his income was used to pay their loan instalments and household expenses, while her income was saved.

Though her husband handles the finances, Sadani keeps herself informed about what's going where, and knows how much she has in tax-saving instruments and how much in liquid cash. When she was working, she had also invested in a post-office monthly income scheme, and the regular interest income from that has been invested in a systematic investment plan of an equity mutual fund.

Sadani says, "We ensured that higher risk investments and repayment of housing loan were made from my husband's income so that in the future, if I decided not to work at all, the obligations could still be met by his income." So, she has been able to effortlessly slip into the role of full-time mother, without the family compromising too much on expenses. However, Sadani hopes to rejoin the workforce once her son is a little older.

Old Age Blues

"Since women, on an average, live longer than men, a financial plan with a cash flow that would last longer than an average man's life should be created," says Binayak Dutta, chief, sales and distribution, Prudential ICICI Life Insurance. In urban India, women tend to outlive men by at least five years and the financial plan of the family should factor this.

Longer lifespan. Life expectancy has gone up in the past decade, and retirement planning is only now beginning to take root. Women are just beginning to understand the importance of starting retirement planning early and not procrastinating on it. "Saving for a retirement corpus should begin on your first day at work," advises Jhaveri.

An early start is essential because money needs time to grow. A healthy retirement portfolio should include growth investments like stocks, equity mutual funds and real estate. Living longer also means that the woman's retirement fund must provide a regular income and cover her health expenses. This could come from annuities from life insurance companies, particularly those that provide regular income to the surviving spouse.

Well, you may say, I've got pension, so I don't need to save for retirement. Sadly, most women cannot say the same. And even if they do get pension, it is often not enough to maintain their regular standard of living. Adds Kanwar: "Less than half the total number of working women participate in pension plans. So, investing prudently to meet long-term financial goals becomes imperative."

Comfortable retirement. What all this means is that you must plan your family finances in such a way that a comfortable retired life is assured. Take the case of the Kapurs. Rita's monthly pension is meagre. Her husband's larger pension is used to meet household expenses, supplemented by their income from investments in the post-office monthly income scheme and Senior Citizen's Savings Scheme.

Apart from this, Kapur has her own PPF account to ensure that future needs are met. What will make Kapurs' retirement fund grow are their investments in stocks, some of them blue chip.

But how will the Kapurs tackle rising healthcare expenses? Rita is entitled to treatment at Central Government Health Scheme centres and reimbursements at CGHS rates. Since this will not suffice, savings will need to supplement them. Clearly, most of this family's bases are covered.

And though Rita does not take an active interest in managing the family's finances, she is reasonably well informed about what money is invested where. That will go a long way in making her sunset years easy.

Challenges for the single woman. How should women who choose to stay single or who are divorced and without kids plan for their retirement? Ask Delhi's author and publisher, Urvashi Butalia, 54, a single woman. "Saving is extremely important for single women," she says.

"Though we might not have the same anxieties such as saving for children's future, the insecurities are far greater. We have to be self-reliant in an emergency or in the sunset years." Financial planning has become more difficult for Butalia since she moved from being an academic to an author-publisher.

Butalia also needs to take care of her mother, who is 80. For her sunset years, she has invested mostly in tax-saving options such as PPF and NSC, besides putting away some money in fixed deposits. She subscribed to some IPOs recently and has also invested in a plot of land. Butalia manages her mother's post-office saving schemes to ensure that there's a regular income from them.

Wealth Transfer

If the plan calls for the assets to be transferred to the children, the woman should know that she has been left comfortably off and will not have to depend on the kids. As supervisor to the estate plan, she should be able to make sure the transfer of assets happens smoothly.

An effective estate plan must be made by the couple and not just by one person. The Kapurs show how a couple can actively manage a joint estate plan.

"We have a diary in which all the details of our investments are listed," says Kapur. This can be a useful ready reckoner in case of any emergency. They are also in the process of making a will.

Their son Deepak, 37, and daughter Jyoti, 35, are the heirs of their assets. The senior Kapurs are making an effort to ensure that the distribution of assets is equitable. An estate plan is also necessary for single women to ensure that their assets go to their loved ones or to a cherished cause.

Retirement, Pensions, and Income for U.S. Women

- The estimated age at retirement for women, 1995–2000, was 61.4 years of age.

- Of the 60 million wage and salaried women working in June 2002, just 47 percent participated in a retirement plan. Remember, even small amounts can earn interest and add up over time.

- On average a female retiring at age 55 can expect to live another 27[frac12] years. Savings can increase a woman's chances of having enough money to last during her retirement.

- Fewer women than men receive pensions when they retire with only 28.5 percent of all women today age 65 and older receiving pension income.

- Women are more likely to work in part-time jobs that don't qualify for a retirement plan. And working women are more likely than men to interrupt their careers to take care of family members; they work fewer years and contribute less toward their retirement. If you work and if you qualify, join a retirement plan now.

- By and large, women invest more conservatively than men and receive lower rates of return from their investments over time. Choose carefully where you put your money and learn how to make your investments grow.

- In 2004, the median income for women age 55 to 64 was $20,810; for women age 65 and over, it was $12,080. The corresponding figures for men in these age groups are nearly twice as high—$39,212 and $21,102, respectively.

U.S. Department of Labor, Women's Bureau,
www.dol.gov, April 17, 2007.

Sharad Mohan, marketing director, retail banking, Citibank NA, says, "Women tend to be more adept at managing short-term transactions such as balancing the inflows and outflows linked to running a household or money spent on children's needs." That may be true, but it does not mean that women should stay out of long-term planning.

We would all do well to remember the words of money-wise Sophie Tucker, the famous American singer and entertainer who donated most of her wealth to charities in her later life: "From birth to 18, a girl needs good parents. From 18 to 35, she needs good looks. From 35 to 55, a good personality. From 55 on, she needs good cash. I'm saving my money." And so say all of us!

| "The real reason women get paid an enormous percentage less than men: because they're women."

Women Still Earn Less Than Men Because of Sex Discrimination

Evelyn Murphy and E.J. Graff

Evelyn Murphy is the former lieutenant governor of Massachusetts and is co-author with E.J. Graff, senior researcher at the Brandeis Institute for Investigative Journalism, of Getting Even: Why Women Still Don't Get Paid Like Men—and What to Do about It. *In the following viewpoint, they argue that despite advances in education, experience, and opportunities, women still make 23 cents on the dollar less than men. Although many theories have been advanced to explain why this gap persists, Murphy and Graff insist that sex discrimination is the only reason for the disparity.*

As you read, consider the following questions:

1. In 1964, when Congress passed the Civil Rights Act, how much money on the dollar were women making compared to men?

Evelyn Murphy and E.J. Graff, "The Wage Gap: Why Women Are Still Paid Less than Men," *The Boston Globe*, October 9, 2005. Reproduced by permission.

2. According to the authors, how much less does a female college graduate make compared to a male college graduate?

3. In 2002, how much money did American employers pay out in sex discrimination lawsuits?

If you are a woman working full time, you will lose between $700,000 and $2 million over your working lifetime—just because of your sex. Is that fair? No. Can it be stopped? Absolutely.

In 1964, when Congress passed the Civil Rights Act that banned workplace discrimination based on race or sex, women working full time made 59 cents to a full-time working man's dollar. That made sense at the time: As a group, women had less education, less experience, and less opportunity, in part because they were flatly banned from a wide range of occupations. At the time, many people thought the wage gap would close on its own, as the education, experience, and opportunity gaps went away.

But today [2005], 40 years later, the wage gap stands at 23 cents. Women working full time—not part-time, not on maternity leave, not as consultants—still earn only 77 cents to a full-time working man's dollar. That's an enormous gap, and it has been stalled in place for more than a decade. It's not closing on its own. It affects women at every economic level, from waitresses to lawyers, from cashiers to CEOs. Many women have a sneaking suspicion that they're unfairly overlooked and underpaid. But do they realize *how* underpaid?

Lifetime Economic Losses

Let's look at the economic losses a woman will suffer over her lifetime:

A high school graduate loses $700,000. A young woman who graduated from high school last spring and went straight to work would, over her lifetime, make $700,000 less than the young man who graduated next in line.

A college graduate loses $1.2 million. A young woman who graduated from college last spring and went right to work would, over her lifetime, make $1.2 million less than the young man who received his diploma next to her.

A professional school graduate loses $2 million. A young woman who got a degree in business, medicine, or law would, over her lifetime, make $2 million less than the young man at her side.

That graduate may be you. Or she may be your wife, daughter, niece, granddaughter, or friend. Whoever she is, the wage gap will take a heavy toll. That missing 23 cents is a personal loss: vacations not taken or dental work that's put off or health insurance that cannot be afforded.

Few women think this way about the wage gap. Women don't talk about what they should have earned, or how each year's missing lump of money—whether $1,000, $10,000, or $50,000—would have added up over a lifetime. Have you ever heard a woman let herself add up how much she was deprived of overall or how much more her male coworker could afford that she could not?

Surely that attitude is personally sensible: No sane person wants to dwell on what she believes she can't have. But as a nation that believes in fairness, self-reliance, and rewards for hard work, Americans as a whole must consider what the wage gap means for working women's daily lives: the missing retirement fund, the nonexistent car, the precarious mortgage, the food budget that doesn't quite deliver enough fresh produce to the kids. Maybe an unexpected change in financial circumstances—especially the loss of a husband's income through layoffs, divorce, or death—cuts the shoestring on which a woman has been hanging financially, so that she and her children are faced with dire financial choices. Why should families be punished simply because the breadwinner is a woman?

Wage Gap Theories

Precisely because our nation believes so firmly in fairness and personal responsibility, many Americans assume that our workplaces do offer equal opportunities for all. And so, for the last 40 years, most theories about the wage gap have blamed women for underearning. Obviously, the older theory has had to be tossed out: Women earn as many degrees, have roughly as many years on the job, work as hard, and need money just as much as men do. So why do women still get paid less?

The most popular current theory is that women "opt out" of the workforce to have children. Those nonworking moms' nonwages are supposed to bring down women's average wages. But that's not how the wage gap is figured. The wages of women who are staying home with the kids or working part time are not counted in that official Labor Department average: Only full-time workers' wages are added in.

A variant on that theory is that women work less hard once they get pregnant or have children. But is that really true, or are women unfairly penalized just because, for no good reason, their bosses and colleagues assume that female employees can't think both about daycare dropoffs and third-quarter deliverables? Men have children too, after all—and they're rewarded for it, even if their productivity goes down during those early months of late-night feedings. Social scientists have documented a "mommy penalty" and a "daddy bonus" right after a child is born: Women's wages go down, and men's wages go up, simply because they have children. Do women choose a mommy track? Or are they "mommy tracked" against their will—or subtly coerced into accepting less pay while working just as hard?

Let's look at a few other popular theories: Women "choose" lower-paying jobs, because they don't want to do the dirty work that makes more money. But is that true—or are women tracked, without their agreement, into being waitresses or

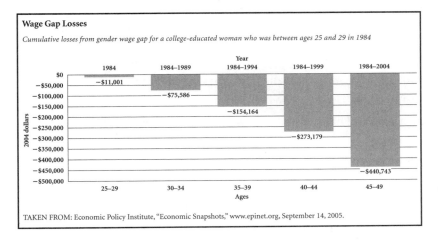

Wage Gap Losses

Cumulative losses from gender wage gap for a college-educated woman who was between ages 25 and 29 in 1984

TAKEN FROM: Economic Policy Institute, "Economic Snapshots," www.epinet.org, September 14, 2005.

cashiers, and refused interviews for those higher-paying slots as journeyman plumber or as bank manager?

Here's another theory: Women don't negotiate as well as men. But are all men born knowing how to negotiate, or do they sweat bullets while they learn?

Here's unsubstantiated theory number four: Women aren't as ambitious as men, and prefer more balanced lives. But who said all men were ambitious? Sure, some women don't want to work 60 or 80 hours a week, and would rather put in their time, do a good job, get paid and promoted fairly, and go home. But that's also true for many men. Meanwhile, plenty of men and women are ambitious, talented, and driven enough to reach the top—but up there, men have an unfair advantage.

The Real Reason

Here's the real reason women get paid an enormous percentage less than men: because they're women. In other words, because of sex discrimination.

Sex discrimination isn't necessarily intentional; much of it happens through mindless bias and careless stereotyping. But however it happens, it's unfair, illegal, and widespread.

Take a look at sex discrimination cases, never before collected, which you can now find at www.wageproject.org. You'll be shocked if you look at how much employers have to pay out each year in sex discrimination cases, through awards or settlements—not 10 or 20 years ago, but in 2002, 2003, 2004, and 2005. These cases show how deeply entrenched discrimination is in every region of the country and every sector of the economy.

Each year, American employers are paying out hundreds of millions of dollars—in 2002, alone, more than $263 million—every year, year after year, for treating women with extraordinary unfairness. Employers still flatly refuse to hire fully qualified women into a wide variety of jobs: forklift drivers, firefighters, salespeople, electricians, regional managers, stockbrokers, senior executives. Or they hire women, but refuse to promote them—as happens to grocery clerks, police officers, university professors, and management analysts.

Think that kind of behavior is impossible in the 21st century United States? Think again. A look at the case files shows that even when men and women have equal experience, responsibilities, and qualifications, employers refuse to pay women equally: as janitors, skilled woodworkers, truck dispatchers, municipal managers, senior scientists. Or they demote or fire women who get pregnant—waitresses, shuttle drivers, sales clerks, executive secretaries, lab researchers, corporate lawyers—even before those women go on maternity leave. Or they refuse to do anything about it when women—nurses, factory workers, Air Force cadets, television producers, bank managers, police officers, deputy attorneys general—are being groped, grabbed, sexually taunted, or assaulted on the job. (While most of us think of sexual harassment as personally repulsive, the reason it's illegal is that sexual harassment damages women's ability to earn a fair day's pay.)

All Women Lose

Every single day, women are being outrageously discriminated against, at every level of the American workforce. Unfair discrimination happens in tiny dentists' offices and in factories that are several city blocks long. It happens in manufacturing, retail, nonprofits, government, finance, education, media, medicine, and law. Unless you look through the WAGE Project database, it's hard to believe how many women are being treated so unfairly that they're driven to sue, even though they know that by doing so they're endangering their paychecks and their careers.

Unfair pay means all women lose. All women—rich and poor, whatever their race or color or native language—are being cheated by wage inequity. Sex discrimination is far more entrenched in the American economy than most people realize. And it won't stop unless, with the help of each other and of sympathetic men, women act. We must prove to American employers that we will not accept the depth and breadth of wage discrimination within our own workplaces. By chipping away at one deeply embedded form of discrimination, we can also tear down bigotry and bias based on race, religion, sexual orientation, age, and physical ability. We can transform America into a society of people who genuinely value and respect one another.

It's been more than a quarter-century since the women's movement brought women fully into the workforce. The time is right for the next step: getting even.

| "The claim that women face widespread
wage discrimination is a myth."

Women Do Not Earn Less Than Men Because of Sex Discrimination

Kate O'Beirne

Kate O'Beirne is the author of Women Who Make the World Worse. *In the following viewpoint she argues that women do not make less than men because of sex discrimination but because they intentionally choose jobs that pay less regardless of gender. In fact, she points out, there are many occupations in which women make more than men, including aerospace engineering and speech pathology. O'Beirne asserts that when women choose their families over their careers, then they naturally make less money than men who are focused solely on their careers.*

As you read, consider the following questions:

1. According to Census Bureau data, how much more money did a college-educated black woman make than a college-educated white woman in 2003?

2. How much more money do women who work part-time make than men who work part-time?

3. How many times more likely are women to get master's degrees in education than men?

Feminists have made the workplace worse by waging an ideological campaign to portray working women as a victimized class, discriminated against in pay and persistently preyed on by male oppressors. Not content with the equal opportunity women presently enjoy, the feminists reject other women's free choices and demand a strict regime to dictate wages.

The persistent fable that women are denied equal pay for equal work has been a never-empty tank of gas that fuels feminism. Since the 1960s, when feminists sported "59 cents" buttons, they have loudly claimed that the disparity between the average wages of men and women is the result of rampant sex discrimination. The demand that people be paid the same salary for doing the same job, regardless of their sex, naturally enjoys broad support. But a sympathetic public is largely unaware that the claim that women face widespread wage discrimination is a myth.

Disparities in wages do exist—but they are largely between women with children, on one hand, and men and single women, on the other. This is not sex discrimination, but rather the result of choices mothers freely make in their desire to balance work and family responsibilities.

Preferential Treatment

Since the Equal Pay Act of 1963, sex discrimination in hiring, promotion, or pay has been illegal. While there might be isolated examples of sex discrimination in the workplace, our competitive economy demonstrably provides equal opportunity for women. But the wage warriors peddle victimhood and demand equal outcomes, regardless of individual priorities and choices. To make the case that women remain victimized, feminists point to average overall male and female wage numbers, rail against a "glass ceiling" that blocks women's ascent to the top ranks of American businesses, and decry "undervalued" women's work that condemns women in predominantly female fields to toiling in a "pink ghetto."

Like so many other female scribes, reporter Rachel Smolkin of the Pittsburgh *Post-Gazette* cited job segregation as strong evidence of sex discrimination in 2001, writing, "Women make up only 1.3 percent of plumbers, pipe fitters and steamfitters and only 1.2 percent of heating, air conditioning and refrigeration mechanics. . . . These occupations offer men with high school educations well-paying opportunities that remain largely closed to women."

Feminist dogma demands that all discrepancies be seen as evidence of sex discrimination that will be eliminated only when women have achieved parity with men in all occupations. So American women, the most accomplished and liberated women in the history of the world, need gender preferences in the 21st century in order to compete. Only preferential treatment will achieve the longed-for goal of having women make up 50 percent of plumbers or pipe fitters.

If it is true that women work for salaries that are 25 percent less than what men with similar educations, skills, and job experiences would earn, American employers are guilty—of violating the law of supply and demand. With a cheap female-only workforce, an employer could bury his competition. (For a time: The resulting competition would bid up the price of female labor until we reached equal pay for equal work—which is what we have now.) Recent Census Bureau data reveal that, in 2003, college-educated black women, on average, earned more than college-educated white women ($41,100 a year versus $37,800). The report didn't raise outraged cries of discrimination against white women. Instead, it offered the uncontroversial explanation that minority women tended to work longer hours, hold more than one job, and take less time off after having a child. But such differences are dismissed out of hand when they apply to the wage gap between men and women.

In a classic example of how feminists ignore evidence against the existence of discrimination in order to make the case that women face bias in the boardroom, authors Suzanne Nossel and Elizabeth Westfall devoted a book to the desperate plight of female lawyers. *Presumed Equal: What America's Top Women Lawyers Really Think About Their Firms* concluded that "systemic forces hold back women's progress and will continue to do so until institutional and societal changes are made," despite women's parity in law-school admissions and success in landing top legal jobs. Yet in Nossel and Westfall's own survey, women associates said that their prospects for promotion were equal to those of their male colleagues, "provided they [were] willing and able to put in the long hours and enormous energy." The attrition rate for women lawyers was admittedly higher than for men, largely owing to "the difficulty of sustaining a law firm career once one has children." The women surveyed by the authors showed "a keen awareness that the women who had achieved the greatest success in their firms did so at considerable cost."

A Matter of Tradeoffs

Many of the women lawyers whose frustrated career aspirations were chronicled by Nossel and Westfall had clearly made personal decisions that affected their lives at the office. These tradeoffs between work and family explain some of the gap between the average wages of men and women, and are responsible for the figures that supposedly show a glass ceiling.

These differences reflect, in part, the different priority men and women place on the demands of their families. In 1991, women without children earned 95 percent of men's salaries when other factors like education levels and experience were taken into account, but mothers, on average, made 75 percent of men's wages. Numerous other studies also find that although marriage doesn't lower earnings, having children does. Being a woman is not in conflict with having a demanding career, but being the kind of devoted wife and mother many women choose to be is. As law professor and author Kingsley Browne notes, "Those individuals, whether male or female, who are inclined toward competition, risk taking, and status seeking are more likely to reach the pinnacle of organizational hierarchies than those who are not."

In *Why Men Earn More*, Warren Farrell shatters the myth of sex discrimination in salary disparities. He pays women the enormous compliment of assuming them capable of understanding the choices that affect salary rates and of taking lessons from the comprehensive jobs data he presents. Farrell provides far more help for working women than the wage warriors' agenda does.

Misleading Data

Farrell explains that in the old days, when he served on the board of the National Organization for Women in New York City, he proudly wore a "59 cents" button, not yet wondering why anyone ever hired a man when women allegedly did the same jobs for far less. While working on his doctorate at New York University, Farrell studied government data that refuted the feminist line. He learned that, as far back as the 1950s, the gap between the average wages of never-married women and never-married men was less than 2 percent. Never-married white women between the ages of 45 and 54 actually earned 106 percent of their never-married white male counterparts in Lucille Ball's day [in the 1950s]. And well over 20 years ago [in the 1980s], men and women were paid equally when they had the same title and the same responsibilities.

One can imagine how lonely Farrell must have felt when, like a good feminist, he was claiming discrimination against women professors but simultaneously discovering that women

Jobs Where Women Earn More

Field	Women's	Men's	How much more women make
Sales engineers	$89,908	$62,660	43%
Statisticians	$49,140	$36,296	35%
Legislators	$43,316	$32,656	33%
Other transportation workers	$43,160	$33,124	30%
Automotive service technicians and mechanics	$40,664	$31,460	29%
Speech-language pathologists	$45,136	$35,048	29%
Library assistants, clerical	$23,608	$18,512	28%
Motion picture projectionists	$35,412	$27,924	27%
Helpers, construction trades	$26,936	$21,736	24%
Funeral services workers	$30,108	$24,492	23%
Motor vehicle operators, all other	$22,412	$18,252	23%
Baggage porters, bellhops and concierges	$26,468	$21,684	22%
Biological technicians	$32,292	$26,364	22%
Telephone operators	$22,152	$18,356	21%
Food batchmakers	$27,872	$23,400	19%
Rolling machine setters, operators, and tenders, metal and plastic	$29,692	$25,064	18%
Financial analysts	$69,004	$58,604	18%
Personal care and service workers, all other	$19,864	$17,160	16%
Meter readers, utilities	$36,348	$31,668	15%
Tool and die makers	$46,228	$40,144	15%

TAKEN FROM: Warren Ferrell, *When Men Earn More: The Startling Truth Behind the Pay Gap—and What Women Can Do About It.* New York: AMACOM, 2005.

professors nationwide who had never married and never published earned 145 percent of their male counterparts' average salary.

He figured that the data showing never-married, educated women earning 117 percent of never-married, educated men's salaries reflected the superior ambition and work ethic of these women. But it wasn't just these educated women who made more than similarly situated men. Census data also told him that women who work part-time make $1.10 for every dollar earned by male part-timers who work the same number of hours.

While Farrell cites the most current data, he notes that, when it comes to examining gender discrimination in the workplace, the books are cooked. "At this moment in history, gender-specific research is funded with a consciousness toward making women in the workplace look equally engaged but unequally paid." He explains that if studies focused on the employment decisions many women make, such as choosing flexible, fulfilling jobs, working fewer hours, declining to move to undesirable locations, or taking more family leave, it would be clear that these preferences explain disparities in average wages.

When Farrell helpfully turns his attention to giving women advice on boosting their earnings, he examines about two dozen causes of the disparity between the average wages of men and women and highlights all the fields where women earn significantly more than men. The 39 occupations where women earn at least 5 percent more than men range from aerospace engineering (111 percent of male wages) to financial analysis (118 percent) to speech pathology (129 percent) to auto repair (129 percent). Over two dozen college majors, including computer engineering, civil engineering, and history, lead to higher pay for women than for their male colleagues. He cites a United Kingdom study that found the choice of college major explained 80 percent of the discrepancy between men's and women's average wages. Farrell notes that "the subjects most popular with women, such as literature and art, are also more likely to leave women unemployed and overeducated." Women are 53 times more likely than men to get master's degrees in education rather than the physical sciences, and this number has increased over the past ten years.

Pretty in Pink

One woman has done more to advance the financial independence of American women than all the theorists, academics, columnists, and counselors who push the agenda of feminist liberation. When Mary Kay Ash died at age 83 in 2001, she left 850,000 sales consultants in 37 countries with both the independence that comes from running their own small businesses and a philosophy of personal achievement that transforms lives. In 1963, after working for 25 years in the man's world of direct sales, Mary Kay, whose father was an invalid, rejected the idea that "God wanted a world in which a woman would have to work fourteen hours a day to support her family, as my mother had done." But she didn't take to the streets, convene a seminar, lobby for legislation, or whine about the male patriarchy. With a $5,000 investment, Mary Kay Ash founded the cosmetics empire that now has over $2 billion in yearly sales. She launched her fleet of pink Cadillacs as the showy status symbols of her vision to provide women with unlimited opportunity for personal and financial success.

Mary Kay Ash counseled that women could "have it all" if they prioritized their lives with God first, family second, and career third. I have witnessed her legacy firsthand. My sister Virginia Rowell is one of the company's most successful consultants. Hundreds of thousands of women have realized Mary Kay's dream. The charitable foundation she created raises money to combat domestic violence and cancers affecting women.

Fortune named Mary Kay Cosmetics one of the "100 Best Companies to Work For in America." Mary Kay told an interviewer in 1996, "As far as I am concerned, our legacy will be that we have helped hundreds of thousands of women find out how great they really are. And that they can do anything in this world they want to do if they want to do it bad enough—and are willing to pay the price."

Mary Kay Ash had the confidence in American women that their supposed feminist champions lack. Unlike the wage warriors who sell victimhood rather than empowerment, this entrepreneurial woman understood and respected the choices women make in balancing work and family—and the sacrifices they make on behalf of their children and the men they love.

"The most promising set of reforms is creating a system of personal retirement accounts within the Social Security system."

Privatizing Social Security Will Benefit Women

Carrie L. Lukas

Carrie L. Lukas is the vice president for policy and economics for the Independent Women's Forum and is the author of The Politically Incorrect Guide to Women, Sex, and Feminism. *In the following viewpoint, a transcript of a speech given at the 2004 College Convention, she argues that Social Security reform is crucial to the economic success of women. She cites three primary problems with Social Security: The funds are being depleted, the benefits are becoming smaller, and all women are not given equal treatment. Lukas proposes the creation of personal retirement accounts as the solution to these problems.*

As you read, consider the following questions:

1. What percentage of women over age 65 depend on Social Security for 90 percent of their retirement income?

Carrie L. Lukas, "Why Women Need Social Security Reform: Speech at College Convention 2004," *Independent Women's Forum*, January 9, 2004. © Copyright 2004 Independent Women's Forum. Reproduced with permission by Independent Women's Forum. www.iwf.org.

2. According to the author, if reform dose not occur, by 2040 what percentage of their paychecks will workers have to pay just to support Social Security?

3. What is the rate of return on money invested into Social Security for a single woman born in 1980?

Social Security is an issue that doesn't just affect the elderly, it affects all of us today.

I am going to focus my remarks on how women are being affected by Social Security. If there is one point that all sides in the Social Security debate agree [on] it is that Social Security is critical for women.

- Women live longer than do men, and have lower incomes during retirement.

- Women take more time out of the workforce than do men, and disproportionately work in jobs that do not offer retirement savings plans.

- Women depend on Social Security for a larger portion of their retirement income than do men. In fact, 27 percent of women over age 65 depend on Social Security for 90 percent of their retirement income.

The actions policymakers take to address Social Security financing problems and to improve its services will have a significant impact on the living standards of American women.

There are three primary problems with Social Security that affect women. I am going to provide an overview of those problems, and then discuss how they can be addressed.

Looming Financial Crisis

The first problem is the one that we all know. The previous speaker already thoroughly described Social Security's looming financial crisis, and its root causes: the growing senior

population, the relatively slow birth rate, and the all important retirement of the baby boom generation. In brief:

- Seniors are a growing portion of the population: In
  1950, just 8.5% of the population was over age 65.
  Today, seniors account for 12.4%; by 2050, they will
  be nearly 21%.

- This means that each young worker must shoulder
  a greater cost of providing for Social Security beneficiaries. In 1960, there were 5 workers paying taxes
  to support each retiree. Today, there are just over 3.
  By 2050, when today's teenagers are getting ready to
  retire, there will be just 2 workers supporting each
  retiree.

- As a result, the amount of money that each worker
  will have to pay to maintain Social Security benefits
  is going to skyrocket. Already, most Americans already pay more in Social Security taxes than they
  do in income taxes. Social Security claims 12.4% of
  each paycheck. By 2040, if Social Security is not
  reformed, workers will have to pay 18% of their
  paychecks or nearly 1 out of every 5 dollars they
  earn just to support Social Security.

These financial problems are particularly important to
women, since women depend more on Social Security during
retirement and make less money during their working lives.
Any benefit cuts or payroll tax increases that are implemented
to prop up the current system will be hard on women.

Benefits Becoming Smaller

The second problem with Social Security is that, even if the
existing system didn't have the financial problems, it would
still be providing a bad deal for its participants. For each generation that passes through the system, the benefits they receive are becoming smaller in relation to the amount they pay
in.

Dual Entitlement Rule

When a woman qualifies for benefits both as a worker in her own right and as a spouse (or surviving spouse) of a worker, she is subject to the "dual entitlement rule." That rule prevents her from collecting both her own retirement benefit and her spousal benefit. Instead, she receives only the larger of the two. And because the typical woman earns less and works fewer years than her husband, 50 percent of her husband's benefits is often larger than the benefits she would be entitled to receive in her own right. Consequently, she receives benefits based on only her husband's earnings—she receives no credit or benefits based on the payroll taxes she has paid. A woman who never worked at all receives exactly the same benefits. . . .

While the dual-entitlement rule has a negative impact on many two-earner couples during their retirement years together, its most pernicious impact is often felt after a husband dies. Social Security's survivor benefit rules can leave widows with up to 50 percent less income than the couple was receiving when the husband was alive. That is one reason why the poverty rate among widows is 19.2 percent, two times greater than among widowers. And, in general, the more of the couple's earnings the widow earned, the smaller the share of the couple's retirement benefit she receives after her husband dies. . . .

Darcy Ann Olsen, "Greater Financial Security
for Women with Personal Retirement Accounts,"
Cato Institute Briefing Papers, www.cato.org, 1998.

This makes Social Security a bad deal for younger workers. The rate of return for a single woman born in 1980 is 1.4%. For a single man it is less than 1%. And it will only get worse if policymakers use benefit cuts or tax increases to deal with Social Security's financial crunch.

Sometimes critics of Social Security reform will try to discount this fact, and say that rates of return aren't important. But for many Americans, this is their only chance to save. This is particularly true for low-income Americans, those who are barely making ends meet from month to month. They are paying more than 1 out of every 10 dollars they earn to the government for Social Security. They are also paying for housing. They are trying to put away money to help their kids go to college.

Sure, ideally they would also set something aside in another retirement vehicle that enables them to accrue real savings so they won't depend solely on Social Security. But that isn't always possible. The money they are paying into Social Security is often their one chance to save for retirement. It seems a terrible disservice that we have created a system that squanders that chance.

This is particularly true for women who often elect to work part-time or in jobs that don't offer retirement plans. It is critical for women that the money that they are putting away for retirement through Social Security is put to good use.

Unfair Treatment

The final problem with Social Security is one that I think should be particularly important to the young women here today. That problem is a problem of fairness in how it treats one woman compared to the next.

Under the existing system, women either receive benefits based on their own work history or as a result of her husband's work history. For example, a woman who never joins the formal workforce and pays no Social Security taxes will receive benefits of 50 percent of her husband's monthly benefit at retirement. As a result, a family in which the husband works and the woman stays home will receive benefits 50 percent higher than they would if the man had been single, even though they paid the same amount into the system.

A married woman who works will receive the higher of either half of her husband's benefits or a payment based on her own work history. As a result, many married women who join the workforce receive no additional benefit for the taxes they pay into the system.

This is not only unfair to working women who receive no additional compensation for their work but it also distorts the decision of women considering entering the workforce. A married woman already faces high marginal tax rates since her income is going to be combined with her husband's. If she expects to get no additional retirement benefits from the payroll taxes she faces, they are another complete loss in terms of income. Plans that increase Social Security's payroll taxes exacerbate this problem and may discourage women from entering the workforce. This makes them more vulnerable to financial ruin if they are widowed or divorced.

I think that an important principle in public policy is that individuals should freely make decisions about their lives without government interference. For the young women in the room, one of the most important decisions you will make is how to balance the trade offs between pursuing a career and raising children. Too often the debate over policy seems to assume that government ought to be encouraging women one way or the other—to either stay at home as full-time moms, or to hit the pavement and work full-time. Unfortunately, Social Security is pretty heavy-handed in encouraging married women to stay home. I believe transforming Social Security to a neutral system, so that it treats all men and all women equally, should be an important policy goal.

Personal Retirement Accounts

I have talked a lot about Social Security's shortcomings. That's the easy part. So how can we fix it so that the system is sustainable, provides a better deal for tomorrow's workers, and treats people more fairly?

The most promising set of reforms is creating a system of personal retirement accounts within the Social Security system. This reform can begin to address each of the problems I have outlined.

There are numerous specific proposals for how to integrate a system of personal accounts into Social Security. However, they share similar principles. Workers would use a portion of the payroll taxes they currently pay to Social Security to fund an account which they would own. Much like participants in a 401k plan, workers would be able to choose from several investment options, such as government bonds or broad mutual funds. These contributions would accumulate throughout the worker's life and would be used to finance his or her future retirement income. Retirees would still receive part of their retirement income from the existing, defined benefit system, but would also receive income from an annuity that would be purchased using the money built up in their personal retirement account.

By replacing part of the pay-as-you-go system with a prefunded system of accounts, policymakers would address Social Security's long-term financing problems and ease the burden on younger workers.

A system of personal accounts would also help address Social Security's second problem, which is providing a valuable program for younger workers. Workers would be able to invest a portion of their payroll taxes in bonds and stocks, both of which typically deliver a higher rate of return than our Social Security system. Even if workers were allowed to save and invest just a fraction of what they earn throughout their lives, they would accrue a considerable nest egg by the time they reach retirement. For example, a worker earning $30,000 who invested 4 percentage points of payroll taxes—less than one third of the total they are putting into Social Security—in a bond portfolio with a rate of return of 4% would accumulate nearly $150,000 after working for 40 years. A woman who worked just five years at the beginning of her life before having kids would accumulate $30,000 just because of those initial contributions and the interest it earns while she stays home. Importantly, this account would be that woman's property, so if she died before age 65, she would be able to pass it on to her loved ones.

This would also make the system more equitable in its treatment of women. Those women who choose to work would be putting more away for retirement. Those who choose to stay at home would still be earning interest on the money they previously invested, but would know that if and when they choose to return to the workforce, they wouldn't just to throw their payroll taxes away.

Trade Offs

Of course, there are challenges that must be addressed when making the transition from the current pay-as-you-go system to a system of personal retirement accounts. Allowing workers to use a portion of the money they currently pay into the system to fund their future retirement means that the government will have less to spend on benefits today. However, there are several ways to pay these transition costs, and in the long run, the government financial picture is significantly improved by making a timely investment in putting Social Security on solid financial footing.

There are trade offs to all the proposals to fix Social Security. Importantly, there are also trade offs for doing [nothing]—primarily that Social Security's problems will simply not go away and will continue to get worse as politicians punt the issue into the future.

As you consider supporting different candidates for president, be sure to ask them how they would address Social Security's problems. Don't just accept their critiques of opponents' plans.

| *"Bush's plan, which relies on private investment accounts and future benefit cuts, will disproportionately harm women."*

Privatizing Social Security Will Not Benefit Women

Mary Hull Caballero

Mary Hull Caballero is the associate editor of the Heinz School Review, *which focuses on public policy issues. In the following viewpoint, she argues that President George W. Bush's plan for privatizing Social Security will harm women because it does not take gender difference into account. She asserts that women have a different relationship with money and investing than men, which could make it especially challenging for them to take charge of their retirement accounts. She also notes the current plan relies more on politics than careful financial principles.*

As you read, consider the following questions:

1. In 2002, what percentage of all adults receiving monthly Social Security benefits were women?

Mary Hull Caballero, "Social Security Reform: How Will Women Fare If Private Accounts Are in the Mix?" *The Heinz School Review*, vol. 2, October 15, 2005. Reproduced by permission. http://journal.heinz.cmu.edu.

2. At the end of 2003, what was the difference between women's and men's average monthly retirement benefits?

3. According to the author, what is one change that could be made to the current Social Security system before private investments are considered?

President Bush's plan to reform Social Security will penalize women, who make up the majority of beneficiaries, because he has failed to analyze the centerpiece of his plan— private investment accounts—from a gender perspective.

The President and his advisors incorrectly assume women and men behave similarly in situations that involve risk-taking, negotiating, saving and investing money, planning for retirement, and partnering with the government. Participation in private investment accounts calls on women to behave in ways that evidence shows they do not feel confident or comfortable. The Government Accountability Office in a 1998 report found that women, who often have less to invest, do so more conservatively than men. They tend to choose low-risk strategies with smaller returns. By opting for a safer investment, a woman could end up with a smaller nest egg than a man even if they invest the same amount, so the existing gap in benefits paid to men and women could widen.

Private investment accounts also perpetuate what scholar Virginia Valian (1999) calls the "accumulation of disadvantage that women incur over the course of their lives." In the context of private accounts, this disadvantage will be compounded not only by their investment behavior, but because they are financially undervalued in the workplace compared to men. Of course, some individual women might benefit from private accounts, but women as a group will be disproportionately harmed by the President's reform plan and more susceptible to economic instability in old age. With the likelihood that the majority of the beneficiaries will find themselves in a weaker financial position in a partially privatized system, any "winners," men or women, will see their gains eroded by higher rates of poverty among the elderly. Add to that other projected deleterious effects on the U.S. economy brought about by the administrative and other costs of privatizing the system, and this reform idea has the potential to make "losers" of us all. . . .

Who Counts on Social Security?

More women rely on Social Security than men. In 2002, more than 50 million people received Social Security benefits, including retirees, survivors, and the disabled. Of all adults receiving monthly Social Security benefits, 57 percent were women, and of those women, 57 percent received retired-worker benefits. About one-fifth of the women received survivors' benefits, which is especially important for women who have not worked in a paid job. Social Security provided at least half the income for 65 percent of the aged overall.

Social Security plays a larger role in retirement income for minorities than for whites. About 75 percent of minority beneficiaries rely on Social Security for at least half their income. Women and minorities rely more on Social Security than white men and receive less in average monthly benefits, because they share several employment realities, including overrepresentation in low-wage jobs, lower labor participation rates, and limited access to other types of income support, such as private-sector pensions.

At the end of 2003, women's average monthly retirement benefit was $798 while the average men's benefit was $1,039. That $241 gap becomes even more significant because elderly women are less likely than men to have additional income from pensions other than Social Security. In 2002, African-American and Hispanic men received higher monthly benefits than all women did in 2003, but averaged about $184 less per month than men in general did in 2003. Also in 2002, African-

American women and Hispanic women received about $147 less than all women did on average in 2003.

Although their monthly benefits fell below that of white men, both women and minorities benefit from the progressive aspects of the Social Security benefit formula used to calculate individual benefits. The formula "replaces a relatively larger proportion of lifetime earnings for people with low earnings than for people with high earnings." The formula also does not penalize women for living longer than men. Unlike private insurance companies that sell retirement annuities (investments that pay out a fixed sum over a pre-determined length of time), Social Security does not penalize women with reduced monthly benefits because they live longer on average than men. Social Security also includes a provision that adjusts monthly benefits to make sure they keep pace with inflation, which means the beneficiary's purchasing power does not decline over time. An aspect of the Social Security benefit formula that has a deleterious effect on women and minorities is its reliance on labor participation over a 35-year span. Social Security averages the taxable earnings of a worker's 35 years of highest earnings in calculating the monthly benefit. Women and minorities generally spend more time out of the workforce for a variety of reasons, so they have fewer years of taxable earnings, so more years with zero earnings are included in their calculations.

In sum, the benefits that accrue to women and minorities in the current program help offset societal factors that limit their employment options during their working years. Even though their monthly average benefit payments are lower than men's, women and minorities enjoy the advantages of a progressive benefit calculation, protection from inflation, and relief from the fear that they will outlive their sources of income. Any reform plans that do not include those protections will put women and minority retirees at a disadvantage. For minority women, those disadvantages will be doubly harsh.

An area that should be studied for potential reform is the current benefit calculation that penalizes women and minorities who are periodically out of the workforce. . . .

Implications for Women

In its final report, the President's Commission to Strengthen Social Security Reform (2001), which offered three models for reform, contends private investment accounts will benefit women in three ways. First, the three models "institute new protections against poverty" by guaranteeing that workers would retire with an income that is 100 to 120 percent of poverty guidelines. Second, two of the models would increase benefits for low-income widows to 75 percent of the total couple's benefit, rather than the 50 to 60 percent they receive in the current system when a spouse dies. Third, divorced women, who must be married 10 years under the current system to receive credit toward benefits based on her husband's earnings, will be eligible to take half of the private investment account accumulated during the marriage. While the Commission can be commended for including issues of such importance to those particular constituencies of women and low-income beneficiaries, its and the President's focus on private investment accounts fails to take into account how gender issues will affect women as a group in a partially privatized system.

Differences in the way men and women view money, government intervention, and risk-taking play a role in how women will fare if private accounts become part of the Social Security system. As it is, women enter retirement now after a lifetime of accumulated disadvantage that leaves them less well off than they should be. Adding private investment accounts to the equation without comprehending gender differences will mean a potentially substantial and disproportionate increase in elderly poor women. That is an even starker reality for women of color, who rely to a greater degree on Social Se-

59

curity for their retirement income than do whites of either gender or men of color. While the current system also does little to ameliorate the societal disadvantages that women face throughout their lives, it makes amends for some of them in its progressive benefit formula. The formula replaces a higher proportion of a low-wage earner's income when he or she retires than it does for higher-earning beneficiaries. . . .

In the Women's Retirement Confidence Survey, non-retired women expressed less confidence than men in having enough savings for long-term care. Lower-income and unmarried women anticipate Social Security being a major source of income. As for saving and investing, the survey found that "overall, men are more likely than women to indicate that they are disciplined at saving and that they are willing to take substantial financial risks for substantial gain." The National Center on Women and Aging (1998) interviewed 500 women across the U.S., all of whom were more than 50 years old and the majority of whom had household incomes greater than $50,000. The results showed that "most midlife and older women lack education in the basics of investing. Although the majority of the women surveyed said they understood certain investments—for instance CDs or Savings Bonds—they knew less about the mutual funds, corporate or municipal bonds, stocks, or annuities."

Not understanding the fine print of an investment decision, such as knowing how a private account will be disbursed once they retire, could be drastic for women. If it is a lump sum payment, she will have to guess correctly how long she will live to make sure she does not consume her account balance too quickly. If it is a lifetime annuity, there could be penalties for women because their life spans are longer than men's, which will again widen the gap in benefits paid to men and women. . . .

Privatization Penalizes Women

Privatization would penalize women because they earn less, live longer and interrupt their working careers more frequently than men. . . .

A Longer Life Means Smaller Benefits. A woman who turned sixty-five in 1997 had an average life expectancy of 19.2 years, compared to 15.6 years for men. Therefore, when she retires and converts her accumulated savings into an annuity, nearly every woman would receive a smaller monthly benefit than a man who has earned the same amount of money in an equally long career. Social Security guarantees the same earnings-based benefits for life, regardless of life expectancy. . . .

Unpaid Leaves. Every worker who takes time out to raise a child or care for an aging parent would suffer reduced benefits upon retirement, because she or he would not have contributed to a personal retirement account during that period. The lion's share of such discontinuous workers will be women. Experts estimate that only 30 percent of women but 60 percent of the men retiring in 2021 will have worked for thirty-eight or more years.

The Century Foundation, "Who's at Risk? How Privatizing Social Security Would Affect Eight Groups of Americans," www.socsec.org/publications.asp?pubid=335, December 2, 1998.

Bush's plan, which relies on private investment accounts and future benefit cuts, will disproportionately harm women for a number of reasons: 1) It does not resolve the system's pending shortfall, which is the reason the President gave for proposing reform in the first place; 2) It violates the basic premise of social insurance, which is a guaranteed basic income that will not run out before the beneficiary dies; 3) It rends the cyclical nature of the current system by pitting the current needs of retired grandparents against the economic advancement of their grandchildren; 4) It offers no explanation about how the transition costs will be paid, which could lead to steep cuts in future benefits; 5) It ignores less drastic adjustments that could resolve the estimated shortfall; 6) It incorrectly assumes that men and women share the same behavioral norms toward risk-taking and money; 7) It likely will widen the gender gap in average monthly benefits between men and women; 8) It assumes beneficiaries are savvy enough to invest funds, when evidence shows most Americans, especially those who are low-income, lack the financial literacy to make good investment choices; and, 9) It is based on political ideology, not on sound financial and budgetary principles. . . .

Any changes to Social Security should enhance the progressive elements of the benefit formula already in place. Real reform should also go further by acknowledging the social conventions that take women out of the workplace to raise children and care for elderly or sick family members. The current benefit formula averages lifetime benefits over 35 years, which undervalues the economic and societal contribution women make because there is not a paycheck attached to their toil once they leave the salaried workplace. The current system essentially taxes motherhood and other forms of care-giving.

There are several options to shore up the system that already have been studied by experts and should be incorporated before adding private investment accounts to the discussion. For example, the cap on taxable earnings could be raised, and should be before any benefit cuts are imposed. This will improve the current regressive nature of the system, which taxes only the first $90,000 of income. While that will also force employers to pay more, it is better to spread the burden throughout the economy than to place it squarely on the backs of those who can least afford to pay.

A discrimination adjustment should be included to account for the accumulation of disadvantages women accrue in the workplace because of gender differences. A discussion of that option would have the added benefit of educating the public about gender schemas. That, in turn, hopefully would lessen the burden of future generations of women, who could retire with sufficient personal savings and assets amassed by being paid honestly and advancing properly throughout their careers.

Periodical Bibliography

The following articles have been selected to supplement the diverse views presented in this chapter.

Vivian Banta — "At the Doorstep of Change," *Women in Business*, July–August 2004.

Jo Casady — "Breaking Through the Roadblocks to Retirement," *Women in Business*, November–December 2005.

Jean Chatzky and Carolyn Bigda — "A Home of Her Own," *Money*, July 2004.

Peter Coy — "How Working Moms Chip In Twice," *Business Week*, April 30, 2007.

Pamela Herd — "Crediting Care or Marriage? Reforming Social Security Family Benefits," *Journal of Gerontology*, January 2006.

Juliene James — "The Equal Pay Act in the Courts: A De Facto White-Collar Exemption," *New York University Law Review*, November 2004.

Je'Caryous Johnson and Sharony Green — "More Money, More Problems," *Essence*, June 2006.

Pat Regnier and Amanda Gengler — "Men Women + Money," *Money*, April 2006.

Andrea Sachs — "Women and Money," *Time*, February 6, 2006.

Hilary Stout — "The New Family Portfolio Manager: Mom," *Wall Street Journal—Eastern Edition*, February 10, 2005.

USA Today — "Private Retirement Accounts Would Benefit Women," April 1, 2005.

USA Today Magazine — "System Cheats Working Women," August 2004.

OPPOSING VIEWPOINTS® SERIES

CHAPTER 2

Are Working Women Discriminated Against in the Workplace?

Chapter Preface

As the battle against the expanding waistlines of Americans intensifies, the effects of this war on fat women in the workplace is troubling. A number of celebrities, including supermodel Tyra Banks, have recently donned fat suits to demonstrate the difficult challenges that overweight and obese women face during interviews and on the job. Although fat discrimination is hard to prove, studies show that it is becoming increasingly common, especially against fat women.

A study by Tennessee State University economists Charles Baum and William Ford shows that obese men and women earn from one to six percent less than normal-weight employees and that fat women's paychecks are hit the hardest. John Cawley, an associate professor in the Department of Policy Analysis and Management at Cornell University, uncovered the same facts. In his study, he found that fat white women were far more likely to be discriminated against in the workplace than any other workers, including fat black women. A study cited in *Tipping the Scales of Justice: Fighting Weight-Based Discrimination* reveals that 16% of employers stated that they would not hire an obese woman under any conditions and that 44% noted that they would only hire obese women under certain circumstances.

Unfortunately, it is difficult to win a fat-discrimination case. In 2002 Jennifer Portnick filed such a case against Jazzercise, Inc. After being recommended for an instructor position by a San Francisco Jazzercise franchise, 240-pound Portnick was denied promotion by the district manager because she did not fit the image that Jazzercise wants its instructors to portray. Despite the fact that Portnick could teach six back-to-back aerobics courses daily and complete other aspects of the job just as well as other instructors, Maureen Brown, director of franchise programs and services, upheld the district manager's decision: "People must believe Jazzercise will help them improve, not just maintain their level of fitness. Instructors must set the example and be the role models for Jazzercise enthusiasts." Although Portnick won her case thanks to help from the San Francisco Human Rights Commission, whose goal is to uphold a law passed in San Francisco that protects the rights of large people and others, the fact that she had to file a lawsuit in the first place says much about the way fat women are perceived in the workplace.

Some employers have argued that they are within their rights not to hire overweight and obese people because of the health risks associated with being fat. After all, Duke University researchers found that severely obese workers had 13 times more lost workdays due to work-related injuries, and their medical claims for those injuries were seven times higher than their thinner co-workers. Ultimately, as the authors in this chapter argue, there is a fine line between employer rights and the rights of workers.

> "It's that issue—the proverbial glass ceiling—that studies find is the most intractable gender inequity in US industries today, despite the gails women have made since the equal-rights era."

The Glass Ceiling Still Exists for Women in the Workplace

Mark Trumball

In the following viewpoint, Mark Trumbell argues that the glass ceiling is still an issue when it comes to women receiving equal pay for work, evident in a lawsuit against Wal-Mart. In addition, Trumbell notes that women are also facing discrimination when it comes to promotions. However, large companies that have such lawsuits filed against them, like Wal-Mart, are rarely found guilty of discrimination because settlements are usually made out of court. Mark Trumbell is the Economics and Business staff writer for The Christian Science Monitor.

As you read, consider the following questions:

1. What does this case revolve around and allege against Wal-Mart?

2. What were the results of the study conducted by Cornell University economists Francine Blau and Jed DeVaro, regarding promotion opportunities?

3. What other companies have settled large discrimination cases out of court?

A lawsuit against America's largest employer is serving as a reminder that concerns about gender discrimination persist, despite four decades of focus on equal workplace rights.

Wal-Mart hasn't been found guilty of sex discrimination— and it may never be, in part because class-action cases on this issue are often settled out of court.

But the very fact that such a large case against the retailer has made it this far—with a federal appeals court giving the go-ahead Tuesday [February 6, 2007] for a class-action lawsuit involving more than 1.5 million women—puts the issue back in the national spotlight more than any other time in recent years.

Equal Pay for Equal Work

The case revolves around wage issues—equal pay for equal work. But it also alleges that Wal-Mart shortchanged female employees on opportunities for promotion.

It's that issue—the proverbial glass ceiling—that studies find is the most intractible gender inequity in US industries today, despite the gains women have made since the equal-rights era.

"There actually has been tremendous progress . . . Women are so much more visible," says Vicky Lovell of the Institute for Women's Policy Research, a nonpartisan research group in Washington. "Yet we do see [discrimination] continuing."

The issue matters not just for women but the whole economy, because the underlying question is whether businesses are making the most productive use of the talent available. Gender discrimination represents a failure involving nearly half the workforce.

Women Face Significant Promotion Gap

Women face a signifcant gap with men in promotion opportunities, according to research published last year by Cornell University economists Francince Blau and Jed DeVaro.

Their data covered 3,500 employers in four US cities. The study found that 10.6 percent of men had received promotions during a four-year period versus 7.6 percent of women—a gap of 3 percentage points.

Even after sifting out a range of possible explanations, including education, skills, and seniority, that gap narrowed a bit, but the promotion rate remained 2.2 percentage points apart.

Interestingly, this study, which drew on survey data from the 1990s, found no solid evidence that those women who were promoted got smaller pay raises than men.

Important Pay Gaps Remain

But some experts say that important pay gaps remain—albeit not as wide as those that existed four decades ago.

"Comparable worth . . . remains a very big question," says Ms. Lovell. She says this isn't just getting the same pay for the same job, but equalizing pay scales across different careers that are comparable in skills and other respects.

In the Wal-Mart case, the plaintiffs allege more basic concerns that the company failed to pay the same rate for women as men in the same jobs.

"I was layaway manager, getting $7.50 an hour" in Vacaville, Calif., says Patricia Surgeson, one of the plaintiffs in the lawsuit. When the company moved her to a new post in the cashier's office, her replacement made nearly twice that much, she recalled in an interview this week.

She also says Wal-Mart made it hard for her to find out about opportunities for promotion. "They would never post

The Stained-Glass Ceiling

The percentage of female seminary students has exploded in the past 35 years, from 4.7% in 1972 to 31% (or roughly 10,470 women) in 2003, and it continues to accelerate 1 to 2 percentage points a year. Yet women make up only about 11% of the nation's clergy. This is not totally unexpected, since more conservative denominations do not ordain women and are exempt on First Amendment grounds from equal-opportunity laws. More startling, however, was a set of data on 15 Protestant denominations in a 1998 study called *Clergy Women: An Uphill Calling*. It showed that even in more liberal fellowships, female clergy tended to be relegated to specialized ministries like music, youth or Bible studies. Those who did achieve pastorhood found it difficult to rise above associate positions, and the lucky few who achieved their own churches frequently had to make do with smaller or financially iffy congregations. Regardless of title, women clergy earned on average 9% less than identically trained men in the same positions.

Adair T. Lummis of the Hartford Seminary in Connecticut, one of Clergy Women's co-authors, says recent, less comprehensive studies suggest that there has been "very little" change since '98, and perhaps even regress, because of what some of her colleagues describe as male backlash. Moreover, female pastors continue to face the same family-juggling issues as their ambitious sisters in other fields, the barbs of conservatives who feel that the Bible abhors their preaching, and the misgivings of a different set of critics who fear that the clergy's feminization will lead to men's evaporation from the pews. The stained-glass ceiling, as it is known, still looms above most of them.

David Van Biema, "Rising Above the Stained-Glass Ceiling,"
Time, June 21, 2004.

the [open] management position," she says. Eventually, in 2001, she left the company and worked as a manager in a clothing store.

Gender Gaps Persist

It remains to be seen whether the details of her experience, and those of other plaintiffs, are borne out in a court of law. The Ninth Circuit Court of Appeals, which rules 2–1 to allow the suit to go forward, said it had no position on those claims, stressing that the decision only affirmed a US district court's ruling to certify Dukex v. Wal-Mart as a class-action suit. Wal-Mart, which says it did not discriminate against its employees, has several legal options.

But the case hints at the factors—some of them unconscious assumptions by both men and women—that makes a gender gap persist even after years of consciousness-raising and diversity workshops.

Ms. Surgeson says her bosses often assumed she wasn't interested in jobs that might require her, as a young mother, to relocate. They would say "you have a family, you can't do that," she recalls.

Some experts say the pay gap may involve factors other than overt discrimination. But many say it's in companies' interest to devote more top-level leadership to the issue.

"If we're going to be competitive, we can't afford to lose women's talent" by failing to promote them on their merit, says Sharlene Hesse-Biber, a Boston College sociologist and author of "Working Women in America: Split Dreams."

Settling Out of Court

Wal-Mart says it will challenge Tuesday's ruling by asking the Ninth Circuit to rehear the case. "The panel's decision contradicts numerous decisions from the Supreme Court and the Ninth District itself," attorney Theodore Boutrous Jr., Wal-Mart's lead counsel for the appeal, said in a statement. "The plaintiffs' lawyers persuaded the panel to accept a theory that would force employers to make decisions based on statistics, not merit, and would deny employers their basic due process rights."

Critics of the class-action suit also question, among other things, the unprecedented scale of this workplace gender-rights case.

"It's basically extortionist," Robin Conrad, a vice president with the US Chamber of Commerce, told the Associated Press. If it stands, it likely would force Wal-Mart to settle out of court than risk losing at trial.

Most large discrimination cases are settled out of court. Home Depot settled a sex-discrimination class-action suit in 1997 for $104 million. That same year, Publix Super Markets paid $81.5 million for discriminating against female workers.

> *"Feminism went a long way toward shattering the glass ceilings that limited [women's] prospects outside the home. Now the glass ceiling begins at home."*

The Real Glass Ceiling Begins at Home

Linda Hirshman

Linda Hirshman is a retired women's studies professor from Brandeis University and the author of Get to Work: A Manifesto for Women of the World. *In the following viewpoint, she argues that although discrimination against women in the workplace does exist, the real glass ceiling begins at home. Feminists have not spent enough time critiquing the unequal balance of power in the domestic arena; therefore, women are being held back from career success because of home life demands. Hirshman offers a plan for overcoming this barrier that begins in college and ends with choices about child-rearing.*

As you read, consider the following questions:

1. What percentage of the women in the author's study were not working full-time when she interviewed them in 2003 and 2004?

2. According to the author, what are the three rules for helping women overcome the glass ceiling at home?

3. According to Phyllis Moen and Patricia Roehling, when couples marry, how much more time does a woman spend doing housework?

Half the wealthiest, most-privileged, best-educated females in the country stay home with their babies rather than work in the market economy. . . .

I stumbled across the news three years ago when researching a book on marriage after feminism. I found that among the educated elite, who are the logical heirs of the agenda of empowering women, feminism has largely failed in its goals. There are few women in the corridors of power, and marriage is essentially unchanged. The number of women at universities exceeds the number of men. But, more than a generation after feminism, the number of women in elite jobs doesn't come close.

Why did this happen? The answer I discovered—an answer neither feminist leaders nor women themselves want to face—is that while the public world has changed, albeit imperfectly, to accommodate women among the elite, private lives have hardly budged. The real glass ceiling is at home.

Looking back, it seems obvious that the unreconstructed family was destined to re-emerge after the passage of feminism's storm of social change. Following the original impulse to address everything in the lives of women, feminism turned its focus to cracking open the doors of the public power structure. This was no small task. At the beginning, there were male juries and male Ivy League schools, sexsegregated want ads, discriminatory employers, harassing colleagues. As a result of feminist efforts—and larger economic trends—the percentage of women, even of mothers in full- or part-time employment, rose robustly through the 1980s and early '90s.

But then the pace slowed. The census numbers for all working mothers leveled off around 1990 and have fallen modestly since 1998. In interviews, women with enough money to quit work say they are "choosing" to opt out. Their words conceal a crucial reality: the belief that women are responsible for child-rearing and homemaking was largely untouched by decades of workplace feminism. Add to this the good evidence that the upper-class workplace has become more demanding and then mix in the successful conservative cultural campaign to reinforce traditional gender roles and you've got a perfect recipe for feminism's stall . . .

The "Sunday Styles" Study

I stumbled across the story when, while planning a book, I happened to watch *Sex and The City*'s Charlotte agonize about getting her wedding announcement in the "Sunday Styles" section of the *New York Times*. What better sample, I thought, than the brilliantly educated and accomplished brides of the "Sunday Styles," circa 1996? At marriage, they included a vice president of client communication, a gastroenterologist, a lawyer, an editor, and a marketing executive. In 2003 and 2004, I tracked them down and called them. I interviewed about 80 percent of the 41 women who announced their weddings over three Sundays in 1996. Around 40 years old, college graduates with careers: Who was more likely than they to be reaping feminism's promise of opportunity? Imagine my shock when I found almost all the brides from the first Sunday at home with their children. Statistical anomaly? Nope. Same result for the next Sunday. And the one after that.

Ninety percent of the brides I found had had babies. Of the 30 with babies, five were still working full time. Twenty-five, or 85 percent were not working full time. Of those not working full time, 10 were working part time but often a long way from their prior career paths. And half the married women with children were not working at all. . . .

It is possible that the workplace is discriminatory and hostile to family life. If firms had hired every childless woman lawyer available, that alone would have been enough to raise the percentage of female law partners above 16 percent in 30 years. It is also possible that women are voluntarily taking themselves out of the elite job competition for lower status and lower-paying jobs. Women must take responsibility for the consequences of their decisions. It defies reason to claim that the falloff from 40 percent of the class at law school to 16 percent of the partners at all the big law firms is unrelated to half the mothers with graduate and professional degrees leaving full-time work at childbirth and staying away for several years after that, or possibly bidding down.

This isn't only about day care. Half my *Times* brides quit *before* the first baby came. In interviews, at least half of them expressed a hope never to work again. None had realistic plans to work. More importantly, when they quit, they were already alienated from their work or at least not committed to a life of work. One, a female MBA, said she could never figure out why the men at her workplace, which fired her, were so excited about making deals. "It's only money," she mused. Not surprisingly, even where employers offered them part-time work, they were not interested in taking it.

The Failure of Choice Feminism

What is going on? Most women hope to marry and have babies. If they resist the traditional female responsibilities of child-rearing and householding, what Arlie Hochschild called "The Second Shift," they are fixing for a fight. But elite women aren't resisting tradition. None of the stay-at-home brides I interviewed saw the second shift as unjust; they agree that the household is women's work. As one lawyer-bride put it in explaining her decision to quit practicing law after four years, "I had a wedding to plan." Another, an Ivy Leaguer with a master's degree, described it in management terms: "He's the

CEO and I'm the CFO. He sees to it that the money rolls in and I decide how to spend it." It's their work, and they must do it perfectly. "We're all in here making fresh apple pie," said one, explaining her reluctance to leave her daughters in order to be interviewed. The family CFO described her activities at home: "I take my [3-year-old] daughter to all the major museums. We go to little movement classes."

Conservatives contend that the dropouts prove that feminism "failed" because it was too radical, because women didn't want what feminism had to offer. In fact, if half or more of feminism's heirs (85 percent of the women in my *Times* sample), are not working seriously, it's because feminism wasn't radical enough: It changed the workplace but it didn't change men, and, more importantly, it didn't fundamentally change how women related to men.

The movement did start out radical. . . .

Thereafter, however, liberal feminists abandoned the judgmental starting point of the movement in favor of offering women "choices." The choice talk spilled over from people trying to avoid saying "abortion," and it provided an irresistible solution to feminists trying to duck the mommy wars. A woman could work, stay home, have 10 children or one, marry or stay single. It all counted as "feminist" as long as she *chose* it. . . .

What Is to Be Done?

Here's the feminist moral analysis that choice avoided: The family—with its repetitious, socially invisible, physical tasks—is a necessary part of life, but it allows fewer opportunities for full human flourishing than public spheres like the market or the government. This less-flourishing sphere is not the natural or moral responsibility only of women. Therefore, assigning it to women is unjust. Women assigning it to themselves is equally unjust. To paraphrase, as Mark Twain said, "A man who chooses not to read is just as ignorant as a man who cannot read." . . .

Women who want to have sex and children with men as well as good work in interesting jobs where they may occasionally wield real social power need guidance, and they need it early. Step one is simply to begin talking about flourishing. In so doing, feminism will be returning to its early, judgmental roots. This may anger some, but it should sound the alarm before the next generation winds up in the same situation. Next, feminists will have to start offering young women not choices and not utopian dreams but *solutions* they can enact on their own. Prying women out of their traditional roles is not going to be easy. It will require rules—rules like those in the widely derided book *The Rules*, which was never about dating but about behavior modification.

There are three rules: Prepare yourself to qualify for good work, treat work seriously, and don't put yourself in a position of unequal resources when you marry.

The preparation stage begins with college. It is shocking to think that girls cut off their options for a public life of work as early as college. But they do. The first pitfall is the liberal-arts curriculum, which women are good at, graduating in higher numbers than men. Although many really successful people start out studying liberal arts, the purpose of a liberal education is not, with the exception of a miniscule number of academic positions, job preparation.

So the first rule is to use your college education with an eye to career goals. . . .

After college comes on-the-job training or further education. Many of my *Times* brides—and grooms—did work when they finished their educations. Here's an anecdote about the difference: One couple, both lawyers, met at a firm. After a few years, the man moved from international business law into international business. The woman quit working altogether. "They told me law school could train you for anything," she told me. "But it doesn't prepare you to go into business. I should have gone to business school." Or rolled over and watched her husband the lawyer using his first few years of work to prepare to go into a related business. Every *Times* groom assumed he had to succeed in business, and was really trying. By contrast, a common thread among the women I interviewed was a self-important idealism about the kinds of intellectual, prestigious, socially meaningful, politics-free jobs worth their incalculably valuable presence. So the second rule is that women must treat the first few years after college as an opportunity to lose their capitalism virginity and prepare for good work, which they will then treat seriously.

The best way to treat work seriously is to find the money. Money is the marker of success in a market economy; it usually accompanies power, and it enables the bearer to wield power, including within the family. Almost without exception, the brides who opted out graduated with roughly the same degrees as their husbands. Yet somewhere along the way the women made decisions in the direction of less money. Part of the problem was idealism; idealism on the career trail usually leads to volunteer work, or indentured servitude in social-service jobs, which is nice but doesn't get you to money. Another big mistake involved changing jobs excessively. Without exception, the brides who eventually went home had much more job turnover than the grooms did. . . .

If you are good at work you are in a position to address the third undertaking: the reproductive household. The rule here is to avoid taking on more than a fair share of the second shift. If this seems coldhearted, consider the survey by the Center for WorkLife Policy. Fully 40 percent of highly qualified women with spouses felt that their husbands create more work around the house than they perform. According to Phyllis Moen and Patricia Roehling's *Career Mystique*, "When couples marry, the amount of time that a woman spends doing housework increases by approximately 17 percent, while a man's decreases by 33 percent." Not a single *Times* groom was a stay-at-home dad. Several of them could hardly wait for

Monday morning to come. None of my *Times* grooms took even brief paternity leave when his children were born.

How to avoid this kind of rut? You can either find a spouse with less social power than you or find one with an ideological commitment to gender equality. Taking the easier path first, marry down. Don't think of this as brutally strategic. If you are devoted to your career goals and would like a man who will support that, you're just doing what men throughout the ages have done: placing a safe bet. . . .

The home-economics trap involves superior female knowledge and superior female sanitation. The solutions are ignorance and dust. Never figure out where the butter is. "Where's the butter?" [film director and writer] Nora Ephron's legendary riff on marriage begins. In it, a man asks the question when looking directly at the butter container in the refrigerator. "Where's the butter?" actually means butter my toast, buy the butter, remember when we're out of butter. Next thing you know you're quitting your job at the law firm because you're so busy managing the butter. If women never start playing the household-manager role, the house will be dirty but the realities of the physical world will trump the pull of gender ideology. Either the other adult in the family will take a hand or the children will grow up with robust immune systems. . . .

Why Do We Care?

The privileged brides of the *Times*—and their husbands— seem happy. Why do we care what they do? After all, most people aren't rich and white and heterosexual, and they couldn't quit working if they wanted to.

We care because what they do is bad for them, is certainly bad for society, and is widely imitated, even by people who never get their weddings in the *Times*. This last is called the "regime effect," and it means that even if women don't quit their jobs for their families, they think they should and feel

Perceptions about Household Contributions

The fact that women still do the majority of housework despite their expanded duties as breadwinners has fueled tensions in millions of homes. But many men have long insisted that they do more than their wives give them credit for. . . .

Bill Rogers and Joan Cummins, a Plymouth, Mich., couple, know the problem all too well. Mr. Rogers does a big chunk of the housework, including shopping, weekday cooking, yardwork and his own laundry, and Ms. Cummins admits she undervalues his role. But so many of the mundane tasks that must be done immediately fall to her, Ms. Cummins says, such as cleaning the kitchen, that she becomes resentful. "It's the everyday things that get under your skin."

When she arrived home one recent day from her job as a bank vice president, she found a dishwasher full of clean dishes needing to be put away and used cups by the sink. "How come you didn't empty the dishwasher?" she asked Mr. Rogers, who arrives home earlier from his job as an insurance agent.

"Well, who cleaned the garage this weekend?" he replied. And their customary argument began. "You never give me credit for anything I do," he told her.

It's clear men are doing more work around the house. Women's average housework time fell by nearly half between 1965 and 1995, to 17.5 hours a week from 30, while men's almost doubled to 10 hours from 4.9 hours, based on a survey of four national studies published in 2000 by the University of Maryland's Suzanne Bianchi and others.

But women still feel more burdened. Many have been raised to care more about the details of housework, causing them to overlook any efforts by their husbands that don't meet their standards.

Sue Shellenbarger, "Men Do More Housework than Women Think,"
Wall Street Journal Online, www.careerjournal.com/columnists/
workfamily/20050520-workfamily.html, May 20, 2005.

guilty about not doing it. That regime effect created the mystique around [Betty Friedan's] *The Feminine Mystique, too.*

As for society, elites supply the labor for the decision-making classes—the senators, the newspaper editors, the research scientists, the entrepreneurs, the policy-makers, and the policy wonks. If the ruling class is overwhelmingly male, the rulers will make mistakes that benefit males, whether from ignorance or from indifference. Media surveys reveal that if only one member of a television show's creative staff is female, the percentage of women on-screen goes up from 36 percent to 42 percent. A world of 84-percent male lawyers and 84-percent female assistants is a different place than one with women in positions of social authority. Think of a big American city with an 86-percent white police force. If role models don't matter, why care about Sandra Day O'Connor? Even if the falloff from peak numbers is small, the leveling off of women in power is a loss of hope for more change. Will there never again be more than one woman on the Supreme Court?

Worse, the behavior tarnishes every female with the knowledge that she is almost never going to be a ruler. Princeton president Shirley Tilghman described the elite colleges' self-image perfectly when she told her freshmen last year that they would be the nation's leaders, and she clearly did not have trophy wives in mind. Why should society spend resources educating women with only a 50-percent return rate on their stated goals? The American Conservative Union carried a column in 2004 recommending that employers stay away from such women or risk going out of business. Good psychological data show that the more women are treated with respect, the more ambition they have. And vice versa. The opt-out revolution is really a downward spiral.

Finally, these choices are bad for women individually. A good life for humans includes the classical standard of using one's capacities for speech and reason in a prudent way, the liberal requirement of having enough autonomy to direct one's own life, and the utilitarian test of doing more good than harm in the world. Measured against these time-tested standards, the expensively educated upper-class moms will be leading lesser lives. At feminism's dawning, two theorists compared gender ideology to a caste system. To borrow their insight, these daughters of the upper classes will be bearing most of the burden of the work always associated with the lowest caste: sweeping and cleaning bodily waste. Not two weeks after the Yalie flap, the *Times* ran a story of moms who were toilet training in infancy by vigilantly watching their babies for signs of excretion 24-7. They have voluntarily become untouchables.

When she sounded the blast that revived the feminist movement 40 years after women received the vote, Betty Friedan spoke of lives of purpose and meaning, better lives and worse lives, and feminism went a long way toward shattering the glass ceilings that limited their prospects outside the home. Now the glass ceiling begins at home. Although it is harder to shatter a ceiling that is also the roof over your head, there is no other choice.

"Motherhood is one of the key triggers for gender discrimination."

Mothers Are Discriminated Against in the Workplace

Eliza Strickland

In the following viewpoint, Eliza Strickland, staff writer for the San Francisco Weekly, *argues that mothers, even more than single women, are being discriminated against in the workplace. Drawing on data from numerous studies and reports, she makes the claim that even when the discrimination is not overt, the lack of flexible schedules and family-friendly legislation makes it difficult for mothers to have successful careers. Nonetheless, activist groups such as MomsRising are working towards ending this kind of discrimination.*

As you read, consider the following questions:

1. According to a Columbia University study, how much on the dollar does a working mother make compared to a man or a childless woman?

2. According to research conducted by Kristin Rowe-Finkbeiner, how many countries guarantee women paid maternity leave?

Eliza Strickland, "Mother's Work," *SF Weekly*, www.sfweekly.com/2006-12-06/news/mother-s-work, December 6, 2006. Reproduced by permission.

3. From 1996 to 2005, how many motherhood-related discrimination cases were filed?

During the summer of 2005, Hilda Turcios was working as a janitor at the Gap's corporate office building at First Street and Harrison, where she cleaned two floors of offices and bathrooms, scrubbing 48 toilets every evening. She was in the second trimester of her pregnancy, and her doctor had recently diagnosed her with preeclampsia, a condition that can kill both mother and fetus. The doctor told her to rest more and work less, instructions that Turcios says she conveyed to the managers at her janitorial company. But they allegedly refused to reduce her work hours or lighten her duties.

Turcios tells her story through an interpreter at the Tenderloin office of Young Workers United, a group that organizes and advocates for low-wage service employees. (The group spearheaded the campaign for paid sick days, a proposition that San Francisco voters passed last month [November 2006].) Turcios, a woman in her 30s with long hair caught up in a ponytail, rolls a stroller back and forth with one hand, trying to placate her wiggly 1-year-old son. Her 4-year-old daughter sprawls on the industrial brown carpet, kept busy with a huge sheet of paper and a box of markers.

Translating from Spanish, the interpreter describes how things came to a crisis when Turcios was eight months pregnant. She was dragging out the trash one evening at work when she felt wetness on her leg. In the bathroom, she discovered that she was bleeding. She wanted to rush to the hospital—but first she called the company office to request permission to leave. "They didn't believe her, and told her to keep working," the interpreter explains. "It was only after a coworker called and told them it was true that they let her go." Turcios says she took a MUNI bus to the hospital, where the doctors performed an emergency Caesarean section, delivering the baby one month early.

Turcios' story has a happy ending: The baby boy in the stroller is the child born prematurely. According to staff members at Young Workers United, Turcios ended up filing a claim stating that the company denied her breaks and forced her to work unpaid overtime, and got a settlement (the staff says they can't reveal the amount). But a new organization is arguing that her individual victory is nothing compared to what the effects could be if the multitude of other working moms who have experienced discrimination were organized and could speak with one voice.

MomsRising

Into this arena steps MomsRising, a new grass-roots political action group that wants to make life easier for working mothers. It was launched this past Mother's Day [May 2006] by the Berkeley-based Joan Blades, one of the co-founders of MoveOn.org and the Seattle writer Kristin Rowe-Finkbeiner.

MomsRising wants to address the obstacles faced by working mothers up and down the socioeconomic spectrum and push legislation to eliminate them. The barriers vary: Some women struggle to keep their jobs while managing pregnancy or child care, while others feel they've been knocked off the leadership track by inflexible work schedules or bias against mothers. Their reactions, however, are strikingly consistent. When women can't be both model employees and stellar moms, they feel frustrated and defeated, and often blame themselves. Rowe-Finkbeiner says they're turning their anger in the wrong direction: "We argue that when this many people are experiencing the same problems at the same time, it's a societal issue, not a personal failing."

There are pre-existing groups that wage similar fights, a couple dozen of which are listed as "allied organizations" on the MomsRising Web site. All of these groups are expressions of the same fed-up feeling; it seems clear that a mothers' movement is afoot, Blades says, and ready to make itself known to mainstream America. But none of the other organizations has Blades, a woman with a sterling reputation, an impressive track record, and a golden Rolodex. (Hillary Clinton's office called *her* to talk about MomsRising and to see if they could work together on family-friendly legislation.)

MomsRising has specific ideas about what must be done. "The reason there is such profound bias against mothers is not that we hate mothers, although some people would argue that, but because we don't have the institutional support that most industrialized nations have," Blades says. Her wish list includes paid family leave across the country; support for flexible work schedules, affordable child care, and after-school programs; and equitable wages for moms. . . .

According to a Columbia University economist, the wage gap between childless women and mothers is now greater than the wage gap between women and men.

The figures suggested to Blades that the problems faced by working moms may be feminism's next frontier. For every dollar that a man earns today, a childless woman earns 90 cents—not perfect equality, but close—while mothers earn 73 cents, on average, and single morns earn 60 cents. These numbers represent disparities in hourly wages, so part-time work schedules and unpaid leaves don't skew the statistics.

"That was my 'a-ha' moment," Blades says. "I started thinking, 'As an organizer, why didn't I know about this? And why aren't people up in arms? And why aren't we organizing around this issue?'" . . .

Lack of Flexible Schedules

[According to] the findings of a recent study by the nonprofit Center for WorkLife Law at UC Hastings College of the Law called "Opt Out or Pushed Out? The Untold Story of Why Women Leave the Workforce[,]" Many professional offices are still designed for the work force of the 1950s, [. . .], in which male employees worked 40-hour weeks year after year, counting on the missus to keep the home fires burning. Today, 72 percent of American mothers work outside the home, yet companies have been slow to adapt to their needs with part-time or flex-time schedules. While companies may see such restructuring as difficult and daunting, MomsRising argues that having family-friendly policies in place will be a competitive advantage in the years to come. Demographers foresee a labor shortage as baby boomers start to retire; companies that can attract and retain skilled women will have a leg up.

Even when businesses do offer part-time or flexible schedules, many women complain that if they accept that option, their bosses consider them less committed and ambitious. One San Francisco woman, who asked to remain anonymous to avoid jeopardizing her job, says she was demoted to a "second-class citizen" at her accounting firm after having her first child in 2004. She was back at her desk eight weeks later, but on a part-time schedule. She says she is no longer asked to participate in office activities like mentoring, recruiting, and marketing for the firm—activities in which prospective partners are expected to excel. She feels lucky to have a part-time position that works for her, she says, but certain things still rankle, like no longer qualifying for holiday pay and not being told about some managerial meetings. Her husband also works reduced hours at his job, the woman notes, but that hasn't hampered his career in the same way. . . .

Mom-Friendly Legislation

[Rowe-Finkbeiner] mentions that 163 countries guarantee women paid maternity leave; the United States and Australia are the only industrialized countries that don't. (California is the exception in the United States, having passed a state law in 2002.) At least 76 countries guarantee that working women can take breaks to breast-feed or to pump breast milk; the United States doesn't. France offers state-subsidized nursery school to all children from ages 2 1/2 months to 6 years. It's probably no coincidence that there are more working women in France than in any other country in Europe: There, 80 percent of women between the ages of 25 and 50 work, 70 percent of them full time.

A number of bills introduced in the U.S. Congress over the past few years seek to imitate the bountiful European system, but most have been shunted into committee and ignored. Many activists keep a hopeful eye on the Balancing Act, which was introduced in the U.S. House of Representatives in 2004 and again in 2005 by Rep. Lynn Woolsey of Marin County. Woolsey knows the challenges of finding work-life balance firsthand; in the 1970s she was a single mom struggling to raise three children on her salary alone, and she eventually went on welfare to make ends meet. Her bill is an extravagant wish list. . . . It includes paid family leave, increased child-care options for low-income families, funding for after-school programs and universal preschool, and encouragement for companies to provide flexible work schedules and ensure certain benefits for part-time workers.

A spokesman for Woolsey said she plans to reintroduce the bill in the coming legislative session, and "is hoping for better results.". . .

Taking Action

As MomsRising has pointed out, even when a woman feels that she's been blatantly discriminated against, it isn't always clear what she should do about it. Helen Huckleberry was employed as a marketing director at a San Francisco technology company in 2000, managing 13 employees and enjoying the work. Then, in quick succession, she got the happy news that she was pregnant and some bad news from her boss. "I was told by an obviously naive manager that I was being removed from my position not because of any performance issues, but because I was pregnant!" she writes in an e-mail.

Pregnancy Discrimination on the Rise

The number of women claiming they've been discriminated against on the job because they're pregnant is soaring even as the birth rate declines.

Pregnancy discrimination complaints filed with the federal Equal Employment Opportunity Commission (EEOC) jumped 39% from fiscal year 1992 to 2003, according to a recent analysis of government data by the Washington-based National Partnership for Women & Families. During that same time, the nation's birthrate dropped 9%.

The surge in pregnancy complaints makes it one of the fastest-growing types of employment discrimination charges filed with the EEOC—outpacing the rise in sexual harassment and sex discrimination claims.

The charges are coming from a range of women, from those in entry-level jobs as well as those in executive suites. Well-known employers that have faced pregnancy-discrimination lawsuits include Wal-Mart, Hooters and Cincinnati Bell.

Employment lawyers say that, in many cases, employers are simply making honest mistakes as they try to understand a variety of federal and state laws governing issues such as pregnancy discrimination and family leave. And they say it's easy to overlook the very real costs of pregnancy to small employers, who may see productivity suffer significantly when women take time off after having a baby.

But pregnant women claim they've been unfairly fired, denied promotions and in some cases urged to terminate pregnancies in order to keep their jobs.

Stephanie Armour, "Pregnant Workers Report Growing Discrimination," USA TODAY, February 17, 2005.

Several days later, she tells the full story at a Starbucks near her home in Pacific Heights [California]. After her manager told her the reason for her demotion, she explains, she met with a human resources representative, who quickly backtracked. "They said, 'Oh no, that's not what he meant,'" she remembers. "They said they were putting me in a different position because they were reorganizing—but that position ended up getting eliminated down the way. They ended up letting me go while I was on maternity leave."

Huckleberry, a petite and chic Asian-American with a bright smile, recalls that she was frustrated, but chose not to dwell on it—she didn't even file a complaint. She stayed home for three years to take care of her two sons, now 3 and 5. She was nervous about going back to work, given that there aren't many marketing positions that offer flexible or part-time schedules, but found a job at a company that fills its ranks with working moms: It banks the fetal-cord blood of newborns for future medical use. She harbors little resentment. "You get over it," she says.

Like Huckleberry, most mothers who experience discrimination at work don't do more than fume. But Huckleberry's case could have been brought to court, says Joan Williams, director of Hastings' Center for WorkLife Law, as could many others. "It's surprising how much goes on that could be presented in court as evidence of gender discrimination," Williams says.

Any employment discrimination case is difficult to win, says Williams, but cases involving pregnancy and motherhood often have blatant statements of bias to back them up. "An astonishingly common pattern is that women are told outright that mothers belong at home," she says. "Employers seem to know enough not to say, 'This is not a suitable job for a woman,' but they appear quite commonly to say, 'This is not a suitable job for a mother.' It's 1970-style discrimination in the new millennium."

Women are starting to sue for more subtle forms of discrimination based on pregnancy or the responsibilities of motherhood. The Center for WorkLife Law tracks and analyzes cases in which women (and a few men) have sued over "family responsibility discrimination." The U.S. Supreme Court ruled on the first such case in 1971, declaring that a company couldn't refuse to hire women with young children when it hired men with young children. Since then, the number of such cases has gradually increased—in the last 10 years (from 1996 to 2005), 481 cases have been filed, compared to 97 cases in the decade before.

"Motherhood is one of the key triggers for gender discrimination," says Williams. "Women do experience problems in the workplace just because they're women—that's the glass ceiling we've all read about. But most women don't get near the glass ceiling, because they're stopped long before by the maternal wall." . . .

Changes to Come

It has been more than 40 years since Betty Friedan's *The Feminine Mystique* goaded a generation of women into examining whether child rearing and housekeeping were the only paths to fulfillment. For decades afterward, career-minded women were so eager to prove that they could do the jobs that they didn't want to ask for any special favors. Joan Williams of the Center for WorkLife Law saw this firsthand. "I became a law professor when I was very often the only woman in the room," she says. "For my generation to insist on new rules was completely impractical. The only issue was whether we would be allowed in to play by the old rules."

The hard work of Williams' generation set up a new status quo. Most women think that hard choices between career and family are simply their lot in life, and don't expect society to change and help them out. Such expectations belong to an earlier era, when feminists piled up victories in legislatures and courts. These days, few remember that Congress passed a bill in 1971 to create universal child care, which would have been free for the poor and eminently affordable for everyone else. President Nixon vetoed it, and the idea dropped out of sight. . . .

One thing that MomsRising can ensure, though, is that if a woman can find time to be pissed off about the unreasonable demands and unfair choices she's confronted with, she can find time to participate in the group's campaigns. "That's one of the reasons for having an online, armchair model of activism," says Rowe-Finkbeiner. "I have a laptop on my kitchen counter, and often do my political activism while cooking dinner, and watching my two kids, and my puppy."

This, then, may be the modern feminist's new look. She has a diaper bag and a breast pump, a laptop next to the blender, a bellyful of thwarted ambition, and a level of outrage that is only beginning to become obvious in mainstream American society. It's somewhat surprising that no one saw the mothers' movement coming: After all, who hasn't cowered before the power and moral authority of an angry mom?

> *"Although an increasing number of companies are offering some sort of paid paternity leave, the vast majority do not."*

Fathers Are Discriminated Against in the Workplace

Jim McGaw

In the following viewpoint, Jim McGraw, editor of the Rhode Island Parents' Paper, *argues that despite federal allowances for paternity leave, fathers are still subtly discriminated against in the workplace. Fear of losing income and career advancement keeps many new fathers from taking advantage of the minimal paternity leave allowances offered by some companies. Although McGraw asserts that bonding is essential to the well-being of fathers and their children, he also urges society not to measure the worth of fathers on whether they take paternity leave. There are other ways of being a good father.*

As you read, consider the following questions:

1. What kind of rights does the FMLA guarantee?

2. According to James A. Levine, about what percentage of men who are eligible for FMLA benefits make formal requests for paternity leave?

Jim McGaw, "Is Paternity Leave Working for Working Dads?" *www.parenthood.com*, 2006. Reproduced by permission.

3. According to a 1991 Catalyst Foundation study,
   what percentage of the 1,500 chief executives polled
   felt that no amount of paternity leave was reasonable?

The federal Family and Medical Leave Act [FMLA] has
given working fathers more opportunities than ever to
take time off to bond with their children, but many men are
still not opting for paternity leave. At the same time, many fa-
thering experts say paternity shouldn't be the sole barometer
for measuring a man's commitment to his family.

Chipper Bro wasn't about to miss out on the opportunity
of a lifetime when his son Nathan was born four years ago.
For him, spending a couple hours with his newborn before
and after work or even taking a few days off wasn't good
enough.

Luckily for Bro, he had the right employer. Patagonia, the
outdoor clothing company in Ventura, Calif., grants employees
up to eight weeks of paid leave when a child is born or
adopted.

"My two months off was the most awesome experience
ever," says Bro, a receptionist at Patagonia. "I got so much out
of it—the bonding, the close relationship I still have now with
my son. Plus, it allowed me to give his mom a break."

Not only was his boss supportive of his decision to take
time off, Bro says it didn't hurt productivity at work or his
job status. "I never did check into work. I never had to."

If Bro's story sounds too good to be true, that's not surprising. Countless studies have shown how both father and
child benefit from early bonding. But due to many factors—
sacrificing income, a strong work ethic or fear of hurting their
careers among them—most men still opt against taking an extended time off to be with their newborns.

Dads and FMLA

To be sure, men have had more opportunities since 1993, when the federal Family and Medical Leave Act (FMLA) was enacted. The FMLA requires any company with 50 or more workers within a 75-mile radius to grant up to 12 weeks of unpaid leave annually to an employee for the birth or adoption of a child, or for other family or personal medical problems. Anyone who's worked at least 1,250 hours for the company in the past year qualifies.

The company must continue paying benefits during the leave and allow the employee back to work at the same or a similar position. The FMLA covers about two-thirds of the labor market and about half of all working fathers in the United States. Some states have their own family leave laws that are more generous than the federal act; check with your company's personnel office for specifics regarding your state's laws.

It's difficult to gauge how many men are taking advantage of FMLA because the Employee Benefits Survey stopped asking about separate provisions for maternity and paternity leave in 1994. According to the National Partnership for Women and Family, an organization that promotes policies to help parents meet the dual demands of work and family, women outnumber men by nearly three to one in the number of parental leaves requested.

But confusing the issue is the fact that only about 15 percent of men eligible under FMLA make a formal request for paternity leave, according to James A. Levine, director of the Fatherhood Project at the New York City-based Families and Work Institute and author of *Working Fathers: New Strategies for Balancing Work and Family*.

Levine says many men resist taking formal leave because they're afraid their managers or co-workers will disapprove.

"Informal or 'underground' leave is still more typical," says Levine, referring to men's practice of accumulating sick or vacation time.

Why Men Don't Take Longer Leaves

Even though most men do take some time off—whether they scrape together sick or vacation time or request a formal leave—many can afford to take only a week off at best. Although an increasing number of companies are offering some sort of paid paternity leave, the vast majority do not and are not required to do so under FMLA—a real conundrum for working fathers who are usually the main breadwinners in the family.

"Many men can't afford to take paternity leave," says Wade Horn, president of the National Fatherhood Initiative, a Maryland-based organization focused on promoting responsible fatherhood. "When that baby comes, most men won't be saying, 'Hey, we've got another mouth to feed so let's give up some income.' It's just the opposite. That's against being financially responsible for most parents."

Bro readily admits he wouldn't have taken any time off had paid leave not been an option. "I am a highly paid receptionist, but not to the tune of taking two months off," says Bro, adding that Nathan's mother is a stay-at-home mom.

A family's economic situation isn't the only reason many men aren't taking longer paternity leaves. Taking a long family leave simply goes against the nature of many men brought up with a strong work ethic, says Henry Biller, a psychology professor at the University of Rhode Island and author of numerous books on fatherhood.

"Work is part of their identity of being a breadwinner," says Biller, adding that many "expectant" men deal with the stress of preparing for a new family member by actually putting in more hours at the office. "They don't work just for the money. (Not working hard) is a threat to their masculinity."

Even when fathers are offered paid leave, they don't always take it. A case in point is the male workforce at Merrill Lynch. The Wall Street powerhouse, which has been responding steadily to its employees' needs over the past decade, now grants 13 weeks of paid paternity leave.

"But most men are taking an average of two weeks even though they're offered more," says Levine. "It could be a number of factors. He may be saying, 'Financially I'll be covered but culturally maybe not.' But it may not even be the stigma thing for them. If there's a mother home, many men simply don't think they need to take leave," says Levine.

More Peer Support

The good news is that the stigma Levine alludes to seems to be fading away in many workplaces. "It used to be that many men were afraid to take it," he says. "We're seeing a shift away from that."

Bud Fishback, a human resources manager at Seattle-based Boeing Co., took off four weeks of unpaid leave in the summer of 1996 to care for his children, then 4 years and 7 months old.

"When our second daughter was born, my wife had 6 months off from work. I essentially took over from her," says Fishback, adding that his colleagues were supportive of his action, including his manager. His time off also didn't affect productivity, as his co-workers showed their support by covering in his absence.

Even a generation gap between co-workers doesn't necessarily mean there will be resentment when a father takes time off. When his two daughters were born, Roger Rousseau of Burlington, Conn., used two weeks of vacation time each. A purchasing agent for UConn Health Center at the time, Rousseau was much younger than his co-workers.

"They didn't know what family leave was," says Rousseau. "To them I was 'new age.' They were used to a guy dropping his wife off at the hospital and then going to the bar until the baby was born. Still, they were very supportive."

Changing Views about Fatherhood

Twenty years ago, dads were little more than an adjunct to the family scene. They disappeared in the morning, worked long hours, paid the bills, and reappeared on weekends. Fearing repercussions at the office, they dared not ask for time off to spend with wives and newborn children. Babies were women's work. . . .

Now, a small but growing number of employers are providing paid paternity leave to fathers. KPMG LLP, Merrill Lynch, J.P. Morgan Chase & Co., Eli Lilly, and Booz Allen Hamilton all have instituted paid leave programs for new fathers in recent years.

Currently [as of 2003], about 13 percent of companies with more than 100 employees offer the benefit, up from just a handful 10 years ago, according to the Families and Work Institute in New York. "We are seeing more young men who are actively parenting," said Kathie Lingle, national work-life director for KPMG LLP, an accounting and tax services firm based in Montvale, N.J. "There has been a general societal shift. They want to be involved."

She noted that 50 percent of the 700 or more male KPMG LLP employees who become fathers each year are relying on the benefit, a far higher percentage than the 5 percent participation at most big firms. Since 1993, about 35 million workers have been granted leaves under the Families and Medical Leave Act, with men making up 42 percent of that figure, according to the US Labor Department. Specialists are hoping the increased demand will encourage more companies to use paid paternity leave and other perks to attract talent.

Diane E. Lewis, "More Firms Offering Paternity Leave,"
Boston Globe, June 22, 2003.

That's important, Levine says, because men are more likely to take leave if they have the support and encouragement from fellow workers. Still, fathers need to take the initiative.

"We should be encouraging more peer support, but men have to step up to the plate individually," says Levine. Many men don't realize how flexible their company is willing to be unless they push the issue.

Indeed, many workplaces have come a long way since 1991, when the Catalyst Foundation in New York City asked 1,500 chief executives what was a reasonable amount of time for a father to take off upon the birth or adoption of a child. Sixty-three percent said "none."

"We are now seeing more and more companies implementing either paid parental leave or extending their paid leave," says Levine.

Beyond Paternity Leave

While paternity leave is a wonderful way for fathers to bond with their babies and to assist in child-rearing duties, experts stress that it's not the only barometer in measuring a father's devotion to his family—far from it. Levine says many in the media are guilty of harping on this one issue; he calls it "paternity leave preoccupation."

Horn agrees. "What (the media) is implicitly saying is, if fathers really wanted to be involved with their kids then they'd be taking paternity leave," he says. "I fear that we're sending the message that this is the only way to be committed, and it's not."

Fathers who are unable to take family leave can still find time to connect with their child before or after work, Biller says. "The bottom line is to spend a couple of hours of quality time with your infant each day and share the responsibilities of basic infant care with Mom. It's a great way to get to know and connect with your baby."

Benefits Shared by All

Dads who chose to take time off can certainly attest to that. Roger Rousseau says it allowed his wife Ann some much needed rest, plus it helped get them both accustomed to their new life. "It allowed us to share some responsibilities of early parenting and gave us a chance to get to know our baby. We got our lives acclimated to a whole new environment. The rules had completely changed," he says.

Bud Fishback says he was grateful for being able to spend time with his kids during his leave. "They grow up so fast and it allowed me to connect with them," he says. "I also developed an appreciation for all the work full-time caregivers do."

Both parent and child reap the benefits of connecting early on, says Levine. "Many studies have shown that children seem to do better in all areas when they have a close relationship with both parents," he says. "And fathers are constantly saying they want a different relationship with their kids than what they had with their own dads."

Bro, for one, is determined to maintain a strong and loving relationship with his son. Reminiscing how he let Nathan stand on his belly, he says the positive repercussions of his paternity leave four years ago are long-lasting. "I can still feel the imprints from his feet," he says.

More Companies Becoming 'Father Friendly'

Although a lengthy paternity leave is not an option for some working fathers, many can take heart in a recent American phenomenon: the rise of the "father-friendly" workplace.

An increasing number of companies offer benefits such as flexible work arrangements, parenting education classes and on-site child care. Moms used to be the primary beneficiaries, but not anymore.

"We're seeing that our members are being sensitive to make sure they're meeting the needs of all their employees. They are being careful not to target messages just to moms," says Cynthia M. Helson, director of communications for Employee Services Management Association in Oak Brook, Ill. The non-profit group has 3,000 members, mostly human resource professionals, representing 10 million employees nationwide.

In fact, given a choice between paternity leave or more flexible work arrangements such as telecommuting, most fathers would probably favor the latter, says James Levine, director of The Fatherhood Project at the Families and Work Institute. "The thing that most fathers and mothers want is flexible scheduling."

Some companies go the extra mile in demonstrating how much they value men's roles as parents. SAS Institute Inc., a software company in Cary, N.C., with 4,000 employees, offers numerous parenting classes and workshops.

"One of the more interesting topics we have is 'Breastfeeding for the Expectant Father,' which explores what your life is going to be like when you have a child who's nursing and how you can help," says Jack Poll, recreation and fitness manager for SAS. "Our educational seminars cover a million and one topics, ranging from child rearing and surviving adolescence to choosing a college. Our male employees attend in the same numbers as the women."

Wade Horn, president of the National Fatherhood Initiative, attributes these new policies to a younger labor market wanting to spend more time with family and the need for companies to retain them. "It's increased our consciousness that it's not just mothers who are valued but fathers, too," says Horn.

Periodical Bibliography

The following articles have been selected to supplement the diverse views presented in this chapter.

Nancy J. Amick and Richard C. Sorenson	"Factors Influencing Women's Perceptions of a Sexually Hostile Workplace," *Journal of Emotional Abuse*, 2004.
Carrie N. Baker	"Race, Class, and Sexual Harassment in the 1970s," *Feminist Studies*, Spring 2004.
Andy Coghlan	"Underpaid, Overworked and Ageing Faster," *New Scientist*, July 22, 2006.
Brad Hershbein	"Milestones in Working Women's Legal History," *Regional Review*, 2005.
Lynn Kennedy	"Belabored Professions: Narratives of African American Working Women," *H-Net Reviews in the Humanities & Social Sciences*, November 2006.
Aisha Labi	"A Steep Hill to Climb," *Chronicle of Higher Education*, October 13, 2006.
Christine A. Littleton	"Working Women: Thank You, You're Unwelcome," *Berkeley Women's Law Journal*, 2004.
Judith Sills	"Catfight in the Boardroom," *Psychology Today*, January–February 2007.
Eve Tahmincioglu	"Pregnant Workers Filing More Complaints of Bias," *New York Times*, September 14, 2003.
Louis Uchitelle	"Gaining Ground on the Wage Front," *New York Times*, December 31, 2004.
Tonya Vinas	"A Place at the Table," *Industry Week/IW*, July 2003.
Women and Environments International Magazine	"Young Women Working," Spring–Summer 2005.

OPPOSING VIEWPOINTS® SERIES

CHAPTER 3

What Can Be Done to Help Working Women Balance Work and Family Life?

Chapter Preface

In an effort to make the workplace more hospitable to working parents, many companies have added family-friendly policies to their benefits packages. Family-friendly polices can include flexible working schedules that allow parents to leave work early to attend their children's plays or sporting events, work-from-home opportunities, and on-site daycare centers. In the early 2000s, some workers have found great success with balancing work and family responsibilities by job sharing.

Job sharing entails two people sharing the responsibilities and the salary of one full-time job. Although there were a few isolated examples of such working arrangements in the early 1990s, the concept did not begin to take hold until later in that decade as more people began to demand that the workplace change to be more accommodating to their home responsibilities. Job-sharing partnerships evolve from many kinds of relationships, including previous co-workers, friends, and even spouses.

Although employers might at first be reluctant to agree to such an arrangement, once they discover the many benefits of job sharing, they often become eager to help employees make it work. When they were being interviewed, Dawn Rosenberg McKay, Kathy Tenenbaum, and Gerri Vopelak of Job Sharing Resources, a company that assists employees and employers in finding job-sharing opportunities, noted that there are many employer benefits to job sharing. They assert that job sharing can do the following:

- Act as a benefit that can be worth money and can be used as an attraction and retention mechanism.
- Enable a company to reach an untapped pool of highly motivated professionals who are using the services of Job Sharing Resources.

- Enable the new employee to get "up to speed" more quickly.
- Act as an incentive for many professionals, since time has become as important as money.
- Help to maintain diversity in the workplace.
- Reward talent and increase job satisfaction.
- Increase morale and productivity. When employees create more balanced lives through job sharing, their anxiety and stress levels are greatly reduced.

Despite these benefits, some employers just cannot see how they can make such an unusual arrangement work. Typically, employers worry that the arrangement is too expensive; that it is more challenging to manage two employees than one; that if job sharing is offered to one person, then other employees may want the option; and that it is too challenging to find good job-sharing partners. Some of these concerns are legitimate. According to WorkOptions.com, one of the most difficult aspects of job sharing is keeping track of which worker does which task. Although they recommend solutions, such as keeping detailed to-do lists, keeping focused is surely a difficulty that must be managed.

Whether job sharing is an answer to the current work/family balance woes debated by the authors in this chapter or simply one of many options that could ease these burdens remains to be seen. In any case, the success of such a unique work situation will depend on both employers and employees working together to do what is best for all.

> *"It is as though Americans are trapped in a time warp, still convinced that women should and will care for children, the elderly, homes and communities."*

Working Women Are Caught in a Work/Life Time Bind

Ruth Rosen

Ruth Rosen is a public policy professor at the University of California at Berkeley. In the following viewpoint, she argues that women still cannot find a balance between work and family responsibilities. Despite the growing number of women entering the workplace, women are still expected to care for children, spouses, and the elderly, which Rosen has dubbed the "care crisis." Although some women have found solutions to this crisis through their employers or the government, most women remain overworked and unappreciated for the two and sometimes three shifts that they work to care for their families.

As you read, consider the following questions:

1. As of 2005, how many women lived below the poverty line?

2. How many countries guarantee maternity leave?

3. How many women participated in the Women's Strike for Equality in 1970?

A baby is born. A child develops a high fever. A spouse breaks a leg. A parent suffers a stroke. These are the events that throw a working woman's delicate balance between work and family into chaos.

Although we read endless stories and reports about the problems faced by working women, we possess inadequate language for what most people view as a private rather than a political problem. "That's life," we tell each other, instead of trying to forge common solutions to these dilemmas.

That's exactly what housewives used to say when they felt unhappy and unfulfilled in the 1950s: "That's life." Although magazines often referred to housewives' unexplained depressions, it took Betty Friedan's 1963 bestseller to turn "the problem that has no name" into a household phrase, "the feminine mystique"—the belief that a woman should find identity and fulfillment exclusively through her family and home.

The great accomplishment of the modern women's movement was to name such private experiences—domestic violence, sexual harassment, economic discrimination, date rape—and turn them into public problems that could be debated, changed by new laws and policies or altered by social customs. That is how the personal became political.

The Care Crisis

Although we have shelves full of books that address work/family problems, we still have not named the burdens that affect most of America's working families.

Call it the care crisis.

For four decades, American women have entered the paid workforce—on men's terms, not their own—yet we have done precious little as a society to restructure the workplace or family life. The consequence of this "stalled revolution," a term coined by sociologist Arlie Hochschild, is a profound "care deficit." A broken healthcare system, which has left 47 million Americans without health coverage, means this care crisis is often a matter of life and death. Today the care crisis has replaced the feminine mystique as women's "problem that has no name." It is the elephant in the room—at home, at work and in national politics—gigantic but ignored.

Three decades after Congress passed comprehensive child-care legislation in 1971—Nixon vetoed it—childcare has simply dropped off the national agenda. And in the intervening years, the political atmosphere has only grown more hostile to the idea of using federal funds to subsidize the lives of working families.

The result? People suffer their private crises alone, without realizing that the care crisis is a problem of national significance. Many young women agonize about how to combine work and family but view the question of how to raise children as a personal dilemma, to which they need to find an individual solution. Most cannot imagine turning it into a political debate. More than a few young women have told me that the lack of affordable childcare has made them reconsider plans to become parents. Annie Tummino, a young feminist active in New York, put it this way: "I feel terrified of the patchwork situation women are forced to rely upon. Many young women are deciding not to have children or waiting until they are well established in their careers." . . .

Women Still Overburdened

It is as though Americans are trapped in a time warp, still convinced that women should and will care for children, the elderly, homes and communities. But of course they can't, now that most women have entered the workforce. In 1950 less than a fifth of mothers with children under age 6 worked in the labor force. By 2000 two-thirds of these mothers worked in the paid labor market.

Men in dual-income couples have increased their participation in household chores and childcare. But women still manage and organize much of family life, returning home after work to a "second shift" of housework and childcare—often compounded by a "third shift," caring for aging parents.

Conservatives typically blame the care crisis on the women's movement for creating the impossible ideal of "having it all." But it was women's magazines and popular writers, not feminists, who created the myth of the Superwoman. Feminists of the 1960s and '70s knew they couldn't do it alone. In fact, they insisted that men share the housework and child-rearing and that government and business subsidize childcare.

A few decades later, America's working women feel burdened and exhausted, desperate for sleep and leisure, but they have made few collective protests for government-funded childcare or family-friendly workplace policies. As American corporations compete for profits through layoffs and outsourcing, most workers hesitate to make waves for fear of losing their jobs.

Single mothers naturally suffer the most from the care crisis. But even families with two working parents face what Hochschild has called a "time bind." Americans' yearly work hours increased by more than three weeks between 1989 and 1996, leaving no time for a balanced life. Parents become overwhelmed and cranky, gulping antacids and sleeping pills, while children feel neglected and volunteerism in community life declines. . . .

Solutions for Some

For the very wealthy, the care crisis is not so dire. They solve their care deficit by hiring full-time nannies or home-care attendants, often from developing countries, to care for their children or parents. The irony is that even as these immigrant women make it easier for well-off Americans to ease their own care burdens, their long hours of paid caregiving often force them to leave their own children with relatives in other countries. They also suffer from extremely low wages, job insecurity and employer exploitation.

Middle- and working-class families, with fewer resources, try to patch together care for their children and aging parents with relatives and baby sitters. The very poor sometimes gain access to federal or state programs for childcare or eldercare; but women who work in the low-wage service sector, without adequate sick leave, generally lose their jobs when children or parents require urgent attention. As of 2005, 21 million women lived below the poverty line—many of them mothers working in these vulnerable situations.

The care crisis starkly exposes how much of the feminist agenda of gender equality remains woefully unfinished. True, some businesses have taken steps to ease the care burden. Every year, *Working Mother* publishes a list of the 100 most "family friendly" companies. In 2000 the magazine reported that companies that had made "significant improvements in 'quality of life' benefits such as telecommuting, onsite childcare, career training, and flextime" were "saving hundreds of thousands of dollars in recruitment in the long run."

Some universities, law firms and hospitals have also made career adjustments for working mothers, but women's career demands still tend to collide with their most intensive child-rearing years. Many women end up feeling they have failed rather than struggled against a setup designed for a male worker with few family responsibilities.

The fact is market fundamentalism—the irrational belief that markets solve all problems—has succeeded in dismantling federal regulations and services but has failed to answer the question, Who will care for America's children and elderly?

As a result, this country's family policies lag far behind those of the rest of the world. A just-released study [as of

2007] by researchers at Harvard and McGill found that of 173 countries studied, 168 guarantee paid maternal leave—with the United States joining Lesotho and Swaziland among the laggards. At least 145 countries mandate paid sick days for short- or long-term illnesses—but not the United States. One hundred thirty-four countries legislate a maximum length for the workweek; not us.

Media Involvement

The media constantly reinforce the conventional wisdom that the care crisis is an individual problem. Books, magazines and newspapers offer American women an endless stream of advice about how to maintain their "balancing act," how to be better organized and more efficient or how to meditate, exercise and pamper themselves to relieve their mounting stress. Missing is the very pragmatic proposal that American society needs new policies that will restructure the workplace and reorganize family life.

Another slew of stories insists that there simply is no problem: Women have gained equality and passed into a postfeminist era. Such claims are hardly new. Ever since 1970 the mainstream media have been pronouncing the death of feminism and reporting that working women have returned home to care for their children. Now such stories describe, based on scraps of anecdotal data, how elite (predominantly white) women are "choosing" to "opt out," ditching their career opportunities in favor of home and children or to care for aging parents. In 2000 Ellen Galinsky, president of the Families and Work Institute in New York, wearily responded to reporters, "I still meet people all the time who believe that the trend has turned, that more women are staying home with their kids, that there are going to be fewer dual-income families. But it's just not true."

Such contentious stories conveniently mask the reality that most women have to work, regardless of their preference.

They also obscure the fact that an absence of quality, affordable childcare and flexible working hours, among other family-friendly policies, greatly contributes to women's so-called "choice" to stay at home.

In the past few years, a series of sensational stories have pitted stay-at-home mothers against "working women" in what the media coyly call the "mommy wars." When the *New York Times* ran a story on the controversy, one woman wrote the editor, "The word 'choice' has been used . . . as a euphemism for unpaid labor, with no job security, no health or vacation benefits and no retirement plans. No wonder men are not clamoring for this 'choice.' Many jobs in the workplace also involve drudgery, but do not leave one financially dependent on another person."

Finding a Balance

Most institutions, in fact, have not implemented policies that support family life. As a result, many women do feel compelled to choose between work and family. In Scandinavian countries, where laws provide for generous parental leave and subsidized childcare, women participate in the labor force at far greater rates than here—evidence that "opting out" is, more often than not, the result of a poverty of acceptable options.

American women who do leave their jobs find that they cannot easily re-enter the labor force. The European Union has established that parents who take a leave from work have a right to return to an equivalent job. Not so in the United States. According to a 2005 study by the Wharton Center for Leadership and Change and the Forte Foundation, those who held advanced degrees in law, medicine or education often faced a frosty reception and found themselves shut out of their careers. In her 2005 book *Bait and Switch*, Barbara Ehrenreich describes how difficult it was for her to find employment as a mid-level manager, despite waving an excellent

Working Mother's 2006 Top Ten List

Since 1989, *Working Mother* magazine has issued a list of the 100 best companies for working mothers. How do companies become the best of the best, the creme de la creme? To muscle their way onto the coveted Top 10, companies must score the highest on our comprehensive application. Our top-ranked companies lead the nation in innovative time-off and maternity leave policies, work/life flexibility and child-care programs. These premier workplaces set new standards for working moms.

1. Abbott
2. Bon Secours Richmond Health System
3. Ernst & Young
4. HSBC-North America
5. IBM
6. JPMorgan Chase
7. Patagonia
8. PricewaterhouseCoopers
9. Principal Financial Group
10. S.C. Johnson & Son

"Insights from the Best of the Best," Working Mother, *www.workingmother.com, 2007.*

résumé at potential employers. "The prohibition on [résumé] gaps is pretty great," she says. "You have to be getting an education or making money for somebody all along, every minute."

Some legislation passed by Congress has exacerbated the care crisis rather than ameliorated it. Consider the 1996 Welfare Reform Act, which eliminated guaranteed welfare, replaced it with Temporary Assistance to Needy Families (TANF) and set a five-year lifetime limit on benefits. Administered by the states, TANF aimed to reduce the number of mothers on welfare rolls, not to reduce poverty.

TANF was supposed to provide self-sufficiency for poor women. But most states forced recipients into unskilled, low-wage jobs, where they joined the working poor. By 2002 one in ten former welfare recipients in seven Midwestern states had become homeless, even though they were now employed.

TANF also disqualified higher education as a work-related activity, which robbed many poor women of an opportunity for upward mobility. Even as the media celebrate highly educated career women who leave their jobs to become stay-at-home moms, TANF requires single mothers to leave their children somewhere, anywhere, so they can fulfill their workfare requirement and receive benefits. TANF issues vouchers that force women to leave their children with dubious childcare providers or baby sitters they have good reasons not to trust.

Unfinished Revolution

Some readers may recall the 1970 Women's Strike for Equality, when up to 50,000 women exuberantly marched down New York's Fifth Avenue to issue three core demands for improving their lives: the right to an abortion, equal pay for equal work and universal childcare. The event received so much media attention that it turned the women's movement into a household word.

A generation later, women activists know how far we are from achieving those goals. Abortion is under serious legal attack, and one-third of American women no longer have access to a provider in the county in which they live. Women still make only 77 percent of what men do for the same job; and after they have a child, they suffer from an additional "mother's wage gap," which shows up in fewer promotions, smaller pensions and lower Social Security benefits. Universal childcare isn't even on the agenda of the Democrats. . . .

The truth is, we're living with the legacy of an unfinished gender revolution. Real equality for women, who increasingly work outside the home, requires that liberals place the care crisis at the core of their agenda and take back "family values" from the right. So far, no presidential candidate has made the care crisis a significant part of his or her political agenda. So it's up to us, the millions of Americans who experience the care crisis every day, to take every opportunity—through electoral campaigns and grassroots activism—to turn "the problem that has no name" into a household word.

"*Preserving and strengthening the FMLA is the very least we can do to protect the health of America's workforce and families.*"

The Family and Medical Leave Act Should Be Expanded

Mothers Movement Online

The Mothers Movement Online (MMO), edited by Judith Stadtman Tucker, was founded in 2003 to serve as an online location for the dissemination of information about issues affecting mothers. In the following viewpoint, the organization argues that the Family Medical Leave Act (FMLA) should be changed only if it means strengthening the current regulations. Although some corporations have complained to the Department of Labor that the FMLA is hurting their businesses, MMO asserts that FMLA is one of a few policies designed to help working mothers and as such must be left alone.

As you read, consider the following questions:

1. Since its implementation in 1993, how many Americans have used the FMLA?

Mothers Movement Online, "Hands Off My FMLA!" *www.mmo.org*, December, 2006. Reproduced by permission.-

2. In 2000, how many employers noted that the employee leaves taken under FMLA had little or no impact on productivity?

3. As of 2006, what percentage of U.S. workers are covered by and eligible for FMLA benefits?

Given the nation's dismal track record on addressing the needs of the changing workforce—the United States is the only economically developed country that does not guarantee universal health care coverage, paid and/or extended job protected childbirth leave, and a minimum number of paid sick and vacation days for full-time workers—it makes perfect (if somewhat sickening) sense that the U.S. Department of Labor is contemplating new restrictions on how and why eligible workers can take time off under the Family and Medical Leave Act. Noting that "the Department has heard a variety of concerns expressed" regarding the regulation and administration of the FMLA, on December 1, 2006, the DOL issued a request for public comments related to the impact of FMLA leave-taking on business operations and outcomes.

Employer Complaints

Describing the FMLA as "one of the most important advances for working families in decades,"—since the Act was implemented in 1993, an estimated 80 million Americans have taken job-protected FMLA leave to take care of their own or family health needs—advocates for working families suspect the primary purpose of the DOL's Request for Information (RFI) is collecting data to substantiate employer demands to scale back the type of health conditions covered by the Act and add regulations to prevent eligible employees from using FMLA leave in small blocks of time.

A close reading of the RFI does little to allay suspicions that the DOL is preparing to bow to anti-FMLA pressures. Although public comments need not address the specific technical information requested by the Department, the issues posed in the notice are heavily weighted toward identifying legal and administrative burdens the FMLA places on employers. Although the purported intent of the RFI is to ascertain "the effectiveness of the current implementing of regulations and the Department's administration of the Act," no information is sought on the health, employment and economic outcomes of workers who take FMLA leave, or for those who need family or medical leave but cannot take it because they do not work for covered establishments, do not meet working-time requirements for eligibility, or who are eligible but cannot afford to take unpaid leave.

While the DOL issue summary focuses almost exclusively on employer grievances, the notice clearly states that employer complaints about the FMLA are not universal or evenly distributed—nor do they target the most common instances of leave-taking. For example, the Department

> "has not received complaints about the use of family leave—i.e., leave for the birth or adoption of a child. Nor do employers for the most part report problems with the use of scheduled intermittent leave as contemplated by the statute, such as when an employee requests leave for medical appointments or medical treatments like chemotherapy. Rather, employers report job disruptions and adverse effects on the workplace when employees take frequent, unscheduled, intermittent leave from work with little or no advance notice to the employer."

Nor are all employers equally likely to report that unforeseen, intermittent leave use is taking a toll on productivity and profits. In 2000, 88 percent of employers in covered establishments with up to 250 employees, and 80 percent in larger establishments, reported that FMLA leave-taking had little or no impact on productivity. Employers were even less likely to report that the use or administration of FMLA leave had a negative effect on profits, with only 7 percent of those in

Synopsis of the Family Medical Leave Act

Covered employers must grant an eligible employee up to a total of 12 workweeks of unpaid leave during any 12-month period for one or more of the following reasons:

- for the birth and care of the newborn child of the employee;

- for placement with the employee of a son or daughter for adoption or foster care;

- to care for an immediate family member (spouse, child, or parent) with a serious health condition; or

- to take medical leave when the employee is unable to work because of a serious health condition.

U.S. Department of Labor, "Compliance Assistance— Family and Medical Leave Act (FMLA)," www.dol.gov, 2007.

larger establishments reporting a large or moderate impact. Tellingly, employers who claim that the use of unplanned, intermittent leave for FMLA-covered reasons is hurting their operations do not perceive the use of unscheduled, intermittent leave by salaried workers as a pressing problem. According to the DOL, "some employers may not even record absences of a couple of hours or less because of the scheduling flexibility afforded to salaried workers, and because the absences often have no impact on such worker's pay and productivity."

Work Disruptions

The prevailing narrative of the conservative business lobby is that a critical mass of irresponsible and under-motivated hourly-paid workers are dragging organizations down by using unscheduled, intermittent leave to avoid work and circumvent requirements for punctuality and attendance. Yet in order to qualify for intermittent FMLA leave, workers must first provide medical certification to confirm they are affected by a covered condition (which employers may reject if they feel the health information provided is incomplete or insufficient). Employers may also require a second medical opinion at the employee's own expense, and—for workers suffering from chronic conditions—may require re-certification every 30 days. Although absences of up to 12 weeks are covered, the FMLA only guarantees unpaid leave—which, for hourly-paid workers, could serve as a strong disincentive for routine abuse.

While abuse of public or employer leave policies is probably inevitable and impossible to prevent, a 2005 industry survey found that only 14 percent of unscheduled absences were attributed to workers' "entitlement mentality" (healthy employees were far more likely to take time off to deal with family issues or personal needs). Human resource experts also see a link between high levels of unscheduled absenteeism and management practices that contribute to low employee morale. It seems entirely possible (and even likely) that in some establishments, a modest number of lower-wage, hourly-paid workers—who, according to the latest work-life research, are least likely of all workers to have control over their working time and location—are using FMLA leave to mitigate the inflexibility of their working conditions without losing their jobs and health coverage. Referring to a national survey which found that less than 1 percent of all workers in covered establishments take unscheduled, intermittent FMLA leave, the RFI does question whether "the temporary absence of less than 1 in 135 employees" has "a significant impact on the overall efficiency of most employers' operations." But from the nature of the employer-controlled data requested by the Department, it appears that one of the principal objectives of the Request is to determine whether the actual incidence of unscheduled, intermittent FMLA leave-taking is significantly underestimated—which would lend credibility to charges that the negative impact of leave-taking on businesses is more severe than government data implies.

Yet a quick survey of FMLA-related testimony and public comments on the U. S. Chamber of Commerce web site reveals a small but powerful group of employers reciting anecdotal evidence and individual examples of problematic leave-taking. A prevalent complaint among employers is that FMLA regulations interfere with programs to motivate workers by giving awards for perfect attendance—hardly a ruinous development, considering that leaders in the human resource field rate "personal recognition" programs the least effective strategy for reducing absenteeism. Although anti-FMLA employers often suggest that worker entitlements under the Act constrain managers' ability to reassign or discipline problem employees, the DOL observes that "some believe the apparent concentration of workers taking unscheduled, intermittent leave [in particular establishments or facilities] may be due to poor management or labor relations problems." In other words, it's quite possible that the productivity and profit loss reported by employers cannot be attributed to the FMLA as it is presently regulated and administered, but is a reflection the failure of some employers to adapt to realities of the 21st century workforce.

Meanwhile, new research on the relationship between parental leave and healthy child development indicates that longer, paid leaves are associated with better infant outcomes, but shorter, unpaid leaves are not. If any modifications are in store for the FMLA, it should be to expand FMLA coverage to more workers (currently, around 60 percent of U.S. workers are both covered and eligible), extend the duration of leave from a maximum of 12 to a minimum of 16 weeks, and provide wage replacement for workers who need longer, continuous leaves for childbirth and infant care or serious health conditions. Considering exceptionally high rates of infant mortality in the U.S. and the fact that over 50 million U.S.

adults are primary care providers for frail and disabled family members or children with special health needs, preserving and strengthening the FMLA is the very least we can do to protect the health of America's workforce and families.

> "As such, the Coalition strongly opposes
> any expansion of the original FMLA
> legislation."

The Family and Medical Leave Act Should Not Be Expanded

National Coalition to Protect Family Leave

The National Coalition to Protect Family Leave (NCPFL) is a non-partisan group of companies, organizations, and associations dedicated to ensuring that the Family and Medical Leave Act (FMLA) is followed as Congress intended. In the following viewpoint, the organization argues that the FMLA should not be expanded, because it is being abused. According to NCPFL, in the years since the Act went into effect, the meaning of such terms as "serious health condition" has changed considerably, which has led some employees to take advantage of their employers by unfairly claiming their family leave rights.

As you read, consider the following questions:

1. How many times have the FMLA regulations been challenged in court?

2. According to two 2006 surveys by the Society for Human Resource Management, what percentage of

The National Coalition to Protect Family Leave, "Improvements to the FMLA Regulations Are Urgently Needed—Protect FMLA by Clarifying 'Medical Leave' Provisions," *www.protectfamilyleave.org*, 2006. Reproduced by permission.

human resource professionals have experienced challenges in administering the FMLA?

3. According to the Report of the Commission on Leave, what is the most common method used by employers to cover the leave taken by employees under the FMLA?

The National Coalition to Protect Family Leave recognizes the benefits of the Family and Medical Leave Act (FMLA). While the family leave provisions of the FMLA have raised few concerns, employers have experienced challenges with the "medical leave" provisions of the Act. In order to preserve the integrity of the law's leave protections, the medical leave provisions of the Act need to be modified to address inconsistent application and misuse of these particular provisions.

Enacted in 1993, the FMLA allows an employee who has worked at least 1,250 hours during a 12-month period in an organization of 50 or more employees to take up to 12 work weeks of unpaid leave during a 12-month period for the birth or adoption of a child (family leave); the care of a child, spouse, or parent who has a serious health condition; or a serious health condition that prevents the employee from performing the functions of his or her position (medical leave). The congressional intent for "medical leave" was spelled out in the Democratic majority of the House Education and Labor Committee's report which stated that "The term 'serious health condition' is *not intended to cover short-term conditions for which treatment and recovery are very brief.* It is expected that such conditions will fall within even the most modest sick leave policies."

"Medical Leave" Not Working as Intended

The Family and Medical Leave Act has been the subject of contradictory U.S Department of Labor (DOL) opinion letters that have been in conflict with the original intent of the statute, resulting in confusion and problems for employers and employees alike. As a result, employers have struggled both to

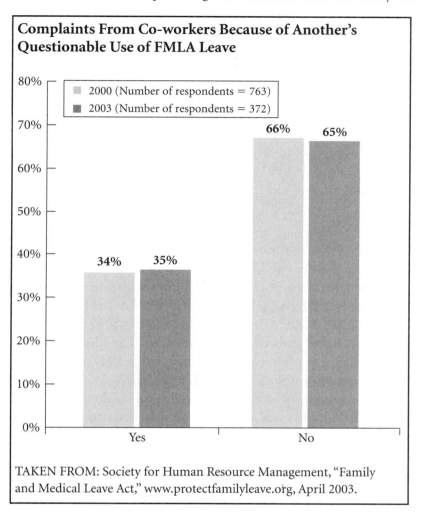

Complaints From Co-workers Because of Another's Questionable Use of FMLA Leave

Legend:
2000 (Number of respondents = 763)
2003 (Number of respondents = 372)

Yes: 34% / 35%
No: 66% / 65%

TAKEN FROM: Society for Human Resource Management, "Family and Medical Leave Act," www.protectfamilyleave.org, April 2003.

understand what constitutes a "serious health condition" as well as with the implications of unscheduled intermittent leave.

While the family leave portions of the FMLA have caused few challenges for employers, the leave for an employee's own serious health condition has been problematic. For example, in 1995 the DOL issued an opinion letter stating that the common cold, flu and non-migraine headaches were *not serious health conditions* (covered under medical leave). The following year the DOL issued another opinion letter stating that *these maladies might be considered serious health conditions.* As a result of these inconsistent interpretations, almost anything, after three days and a doctor's visit, now qualifies as a serious medical condition. Employers aren't sure if health problems like pink eye, ingrown toenails—even the common cold—will be considered by the regulators and courts to be "serious" health conditions.

The "intermittent leave" regulations, coupled with the vague "serious health conditions" regulations, allow employees to characterize chronic, non-serious health conditions as FMLA leave. This misuse of FMLA leave threatens the integrity of this important law for those employees who truly have serious health conditions. The Act should be clarified so that it works to the benefit of those employees who need it most.

These confusing and contradictory regulations and interpretation letters have led to an explosion of costly and time consuming litigation. The Labor Department's FMLA regulations have been challenged in over 70 court decisions and even the U.S. Supreme Court has found one FMLA regulation to be "contrary to the Act's remedial design."

Finally, recent survey efforts have highlighted the challenges HR professionals and employers experience in administering the medical leave provisions of the FMLA. According to the Society for Human Resource Management (SHRM) Weekly Surveys on November 7 and November 15, 2006:

- 51 percent of HR professionals have experienced challenges in administering/granting leave under the FMLA for an employee's serious health condition.

- 47 percent of respondents cited challenges in granting FMLA leave for chronic conditions, versus 11 percent for a catastrophic event.

- Specific problems encountered due to employees taking FMLA leave as a result of a chronic condition included:

- 69 percent: Tracking intermittent leave

- 66 percent: Vague documentation of medical leave certification

- 66 percent: Chronic abuse of intermittent leave by employees

- 66 percent: Unsure about the legitimacy of leave requests

FMLA Hurts Conscientious Employees

The greatest cost of the FMLA is the cost to employees themselves. The Report of the Commission on Leave, mandated by the Act, found that "by far the most prevalent method that employers use to cover work is to assign it temporarily to other coworkers (67%)." Similar results were reported in the Society for Human Resource Management 2003 Family and Medical Leave Act Survey report. HR professionals responding to the survey suggested that "assigning work temporarily to other employees" was the most used method for attending to an FMLA employee's workload. This means that employees who are not taking leave under the FMLA are being forced to absorb the extra workload from those who are. As a result of the permissive and confusing FMLA regulations, increasingly, leave is being taken with little or no notice, requiring unscheduled overtime by coworkers.

The FMLA Solution

The National Coalition to Protect Family Leave has repeatedly urged the DOL and the United States Congress to strengthen the FMLA by clarifying the medical leave interpretations and other FMLA administrative complexities which are causing problems in the workplace. The Coalition supports technical corrections through either regulations or legislation that will ensure implementation of the law consistent with the intent of Congress as expressed in the House Committee report. These technical corrections include:

- restoring the meaning of "serious health condition" to the original congressional intent;

- improving notification requirements to reduce work disruptions and shifting unwanted overtime to employees;

- streamlining record keeping; and

- allowing employers to offer a choice between FMLA benefits or paid sick-leave.

Furthermore, the Coalition believes that these issues need to be addressed before Congress considers expanding the Act. As such, the Coalition strongly opposes any expansion of the original FMLA legislation. Expanding a law that is not working properly will only exacerbate the problems that employees and employers are having under the law's misapplication.

| *"Care for children of families with incomes at or below the poverty line should be subsidized completely out of public funds."*

The Federal Government Should Subsidize Child Care

Suzanne W. Helburn and Barbara Bergmann

Suzanne Wiggans Helburn is professor emerita of economics at the University of Colorado, Denver, and Barbara R. Bergman is professor emerita of economics at the University of Maryland. In the following viewpoint, they argue that the federal government must contribute the most money towards childcare. Although they recommend that state and local governments manage these funds, they assert that U.S. children and their families will continue to go without quality, affordable childcare until the federal government expands its current programs.

As you read, consider the following questions:

1. How much would the childcare program proposed by the authors cost the federal government per year?

Suzanne W. Helburn and Barbara Bergman, *America's Child Care Problem: The Way Out*. Basingstoke, Hampshire: Palgrave MacMillan, 2003. Copyright © Barbara Bergmann and Suzanne Helburn 2002. All rights reserved. Reproduced with permission of Palgrave Macmillan Ltd.

2. According to the authors, parents' childcare budget should be no more than what percentage of their income above the poverty line?

3. According to the authors, in what two ways will employers gain from their childcare proposal?

The American child care system, in which parents, largely unassisted, must buy the care they need in the marketplace, has not worked well. It is in the public's interest that the services children receive be of good quality, but millions of parents are unable to pay what standard-quality services currently cost, much less what they would cost if quality were improved. Parents need assistance in two ways. They need more help in meeting the cost of child care. And they need more help in assuring the safety and quality of the care their children get. . . .

We recommend an aggressive assault on the country's child care problem, led by and mostly financed by the federal government but with most of the administration performed by state and local governments and most services given by private-sector providers. Our proposal would solve the affordability problem and would allow us to make progress on the quality problem.

We argue that care for children of families with incomes at or below the poverty line should be subsidized completely out of public funds. Such families cannot afford to spend any of their income for child care; they need all of it for food, clothing, shelter. For families with incomes above the poverty line, we propose the following standard of "affordability": No family should have to lay out for child care more than 20 percent of its income *in excess* of the poverty line. If parents and the public were to share the costs of child care on such a basis, millions of middle-class families would be helped, along with millions of lower-income families. (For example, a married couple with one three-year-old would receive substantial help if their income was less than $40,000 under such a program.) Funding should suffice to cover all families eligible for services who apply for them.

Care for Children under Five

There is currently little direct provision by government of child care for children under five, and therefore a large privately run industry has come into existence. We do not envision the possibility that a substantial move away from private sector provision is likely or necessarily desirable. Whatever the merits and demerits in the use of vouchers for children in the K-12 grades (and we consider the demerits substantial), we do consider vouchers useful in administering a subsidy program for the early care and education of children under five years of age and for before- and after-school programs. They would give parents flexibility in choosing their child care provider.

The providers of care reimbursed under the program we advocate could be for-profit or nonprofit, public or private, religious or secular, home based or center based. We recommend that only licensed providers be eligible to receive reimbursement with public funds. Some caregiving for four-year-olds would take place in the prekindergarten programs that states are currently advancing, and in Head Starts. The move to full-day kindergarten for five-year-olds would provide some additional hours of care, as well as additional hours of activities aimed at getting children ready for the first grade. Children under 13 would have access to before- and after-school programs and summer programs subsidized on the same basis.

Improved Quality

We use the rubric "affordable care of improved quality" rather than "affordable quality care" because we believe a rapid and drastic improvement in child care quality, while eminently desirable, is not a realistic goal given the current state and organization of child care. Affordability can be provided in relatively short order if the will to spend the necessary funds is there. Quality is a more difficult matter. Improving the financial help to parents will allow many to switch their children out of low-cost informal care into licensed care, where the current quality is likely to be better. But raising the quality of existing providers will not be rapid or easy. Slow and gradual progress, under policies designed to encourage such progress is, we believe, the best that can be hoped for in the near term. Making progress on the quality problem would require that the 20 or so states with low standards in the ratio of staff to children amend their requirements. States should also set training requirements for center staff members and for those running family child care homes, where children are cared for in the caretaker's home. We advocate an improved regime of inspection of licensees and less delay in the suspension of those found to be delivering service of less than minimum adequacy. An increase in the number of providers who seek and are granted accreditation and an expansion of resource and referral services would be helpful. Setting up standards that providers must meet in order to receive federal funds would also be desirable.

Efforts to improve quality could not succeed without a flow of funds to pay for the costs to providers of meeting the higher standards. We recommend that reimbursement of providers be at a level that would allow them to deliver services of a quality that is average in the United States today, with higher reimbursement rates for those who demonstrate significantly higher quality. (Providing funds to pay the cost of currently average quality would allow providers delivering quality below the current average enough funds to raise their quality. If such an improvement by the bottom half of providers were to occur, the quality average would, of course, rise accordingly.) The additional funds many providers would receive would enable them to pay higher wages, which would, over time, be expected to increase the supply of trained workers and reduce turnover among them.

Program Costs

The total expenditure such a program would require is, we estimate, about $50 billion a year. The federal government now spends about $15 billion on child care, and the states together spend about $4 billion. So our proposed program would require about $30 billion of new money a year. It would be unrealistic to hope that employers and voluntary philanthropic efforts in each community would suffice to fill the funding gap. Nor can we expect state and local governments, with their limited taxing power, to be able to come forth with the needed resources. Only the federal government would be able to finance a program of this magnitude and insure that children in every community in the country get the care they need.

We recognize that an expensive public program of this magnitude does not accord with the common assumption that "the era of big government is over" and with the seeming widespread acceptance of the idea that the closing of that era was a good thing. Nevertheless, certain large expenditures do from time to time get added to the federal budget. Prescription drug coverage for the elderly was advocated by both candidates in the presidential election of 2000. Additions to the military budget of funds that would be sufficient to pay for much if not all of the child care program we propose is in prospect at this writing [2003]. A much-expanded program of subsidies for child care would not be politically possible without considerable agitation for it, even in an era of budget surplus. Yet polling data indicate that there is already a basis in public opinion for considerably expanded government help with child care, particularly for lower-income working parents; in one recent [2003] poll 63 percent of respondents gave support to increased federal spending to provide child care assistance to working parents.

Powerful opposition will come from those who regard the movement of mothers out of the home and into jobs as a terrible mistake. Yet most people understand that for better or worse the mothers of small children will continue to hold jobs and need child care. Whether mothers "need" to work, want to work, or find that working is the best of all the alternatives open to them, they do and will work. The practical question that faces the country is how to deal with the child care needs that result.

A system built around the principle that parents should have to pay no more than 20 percent of their income above the poverty line for child care of approved quality, if enacted and funded so that all eligibles who sought places in the system could have them, would effectively solve the "affordability" problem. The trend that is evident toward free public provision of full-day kindergarten and prekindergarten, which could provide care and education for children of age four and five, and the increases that have been recently made in appropriations for child care subsidies show that these are popular and politically viable programs.

A program like the one we have outlined should garner support from the public school teachers' unions and the more organized parts of the private child care industry—the for-profit companies and the religious groups that run child care centers. There is a third group, far more powerful than the first two, from which support might also be enlisted: employers. Employers stand to gain in two ways. First, a more reliable child care system would reduce absenteeism and tardiness. Second, employers would be relieved of pressure to provide subsidized child care as a fringe benefit. There is, of course, a fourth group: Parents, many of whom would be relieved of a good portion of the heavy financial pressure that paying for child care involves, and who would be relieved of the anxieties that attend sending one's child to "informal" care of doubtful reliability, quality, and safety.

| *"The case for general subsidies to child-care and for work leaves to employees with young children is . . . weak."*

The Federal Government Should Not Subsidize Child Care

Gary Becker

In the following viewpoint, Gary Becker, professor of economic and sociology at the University of Chicago, argues that the United States should not follow the Scandinavian system of childcare, which provides government funded childcare programs and lengthy leave time for new mothers. Becker asserts that their system simply would not work for the goals established for the American workplace. Given that government-funded childcare programs are often instituted to raise the birthrate, the United States has no need for such provisions given that the birthrate is among the highest among developed countries.

As you read, consider the following questions:

1. What benefits are given to new mothers and fathers in Sweden?

Gary Becker, "Should Governments Subsidize Child Care and Work Leaves?" *www.becker-posner-blog.com*, October 30, 2005, Reproduced by permission of the author.

2. According to the author, what is the most direct and best way to encourage births?

3. Why is France's fertility rate among the highest in Western Europe?

Germany and the United States, among many other countries, have been criticized for not having the extensive system of benefits to parents . . . found throughout Scandinavia and some other countries. For example, the Swedish government not only heavily subsidizes day care activities for young children with working mothers, but also allows up to eighteen months of paid leave to care for a newborn child. These benefits are open to both mothers and fathers, but mothers take practically all leaves. Benefits almost fully compensate for the loss in earnings during the first 12 months of leave, while they offset more than half of earnings during the next 6 months of leave. Also companies have to take their employees back at comparable jobs when they decide to return to work from a child leave.

The many advocates of a Swedish-type childcare system believe it permits mothers of young children to work while guaranteeing that their children have adequate childcare at government-run facilities. At the same time, it allows mothers to care for their young children without losing their jobs. In addition, these subsidies tend to encourage families to have more children since they reduce the cost of having and raising children.

Despite these claims, I believe it would be a mistake for the U.S., Germany, or other countries to emulate the Swedish approach. For starters, middle class and rich families can pay for their own childcare services for young children, such as preschool programs, whether or not the mothers are working. In fact, the majority of such families in the United States do send their young children to day care programs. It is much more efficient to have better off families buy childcare services in a private competitive market than to spend tax revenue on preschool government-run programs for the children of these families. The Swedish childcare system was insightfully criticized along these lines in a controversial but I believe correct analysis by my late colleague Sherwin Rosen.

It could make sense to subsidize the preschool activities of children of poor families since these children may well receive inadequate care without such subsidies. The U.S. takes this approach by only subsidizing preschool care of low-income families. These subsides appropriately take the form of a voucher system rather than government-run pre-school programs. Poor families are in essence given vouchers each month that they can spend on any approved private day care program for young children. The market is highly competitive and I believe works well, although there are few careful evaluations of this system. Still, I believe it provides an example of how a voucher system might work for older children in school.

Leaves of Absence

The case is also weak for following Sweden by providing all women who work with generous and lengthy government-financed paid leaves. The U.S. does not have this system, yet many working women leave their jobs at least temporarily, or work part time, in order to care for their children. The vast majority of parents are very concerned about the well-being of their children, and give that a lot of weight when deciding whether to care for them rather than using preschool programs and other outside help.

Government-financed payments to working mothers who take a leave of absence to care for their young children subsidizes women who work compared to women who decide to stay home full-time to care for children and engage in other activities. It is still controversial whether there is a significant benefit to children from having mothers who stay home to care for them instead of having mothers who work, and care

Who Is Responsible for Child Care?

In announcing the October 23, 1997, White House Conference on Child Care, President Clinton stated, "This nation can and should do better. Each of us—from businesses to religious leaders to policymakers and elected officials—has a responsibility and important stake in making sure that children of all ages have the best possible care available to them." Symptomatic of the problem with Clinton's policy is his list of parties charged with child care—businesses, religious leaders, policymakers, and elected officials. Parents are not on the list.

As child care has moved beyond its traditional confines to include care outside the child's home, policymakers across the political field, from [former] First Lady Hillary Rodham Clinton to Sen. Orrin Hatch (R-Utah), have come to view caring for children as a public responsibility. While the desire to have every child well cared for is commendable, the desire to forcibly take away from parents the responsibility for that care is not. Few issues are more personal than child rearing. Child care should remain safe from government intrusion. Our form of government demands the separation of church and state because religion is a subject of personal conscience and belief. Child care is no more or less personal. It deserves the same protection for the same reasons.

Darcy Olsen, "The Advancing Nanny State:
Why the Government Should Stay Out of Child Care,"
CATO Institute, www.cato.org, October 23, 1997,
www.cato.org/pub_display.php?pub_id=1144.

for their children (perhaps more intensely) only before and after work and on weekends. On the whole, I believe that work decisions are best left to parents without government subsidies or other government involvement.

Raising the Birth Rate

Generous government childcare and work benefits for families with young children are advocated sometimes because they promote larger families. European and some Asian countries are particularly receptive to this argument since their birth rates are so low that their populations would begin to decline soon unless births increased a lot, or they accepted large numbers of immigrants. Yet while the Swedish total fertility rate is quite a bit above that of Germany, Italy, and some other European nations, it is still too low to prevent its population from declining in the near future, despite the world's most generous system of work and child care benefits for families with young children.

This may be because the Swedish-type system promotes larger families in an indirect and inefficient manner. The most direct and best way to encourage births, if that is the goal, is to provide monthly allowances to families that have an additional child. Subsidizing births directly encourages larger families without mainly targeting women who work, or women who value childcare services a lot. Moreover, since the vast majority of families even in Europe have at least one child without government subsidies, an efficient family allowance program should concentrate subsidies on the marginal fertility decision; that is, on second, third, or higher order births that may not happen without subsidies.

France has an extensive and complicated system of direct allowances mainly to families that have more than one child. The best study of the effects of this program shows that it has had a significant effect in raising [the] French birth rate to among the highest in Western Europe, although other factors are also important. However, the system is expensive, and the French total fertility rate is still considerably below its replacement level.

The U.S. does not apparently need any stimulation to family size since its total fertility rate is the highest of any developed country, and it is even above that of many much poorer countries, like China or South Korea. The case for general subsidies to childcare and for work leaves to employees with young children is also weak. So I believe that present American policy in these areas is much better than the Swedish approach, and does not need drastic changes.

> "'Family-friendly' policies ... can provide parents with flexibility and time off that they need to balance their [work and family lives]."

Family-Friendly Policies Help Working Mothers

Heather Boushey

In the following viewpoint, Heather Boushey, economist for the Center for Economic and Policy Research, argues that family-friendly workplace polices that allow for flexible scheduling and paid maternity leave can make a big difference in the lives of working mothers. She points to the lack of family-friendly polices as being partially responsible for the "family gap," the monetary gap that exists between households with children and households without children. Boushey notes that companies cannot support family-friendly polices on their own and so the federal government must complement their efforts with funding and regulations.

As you read, consider the following questions:

1. How much higher are the salaries of mothers who took paid maternity leave than mothers who did not?

Heather Boushey, "Family-Friendly Policies: Boosting Mothers' Wages," *Center for Economic Policy Research*, April 6, 2005, pp. 2–4, 14–5. Reproduced by permission.

2. Over their lifetimes, women earn how much less than men?

3. How much is the estimated cost for the paid parental leave program in Massachusetts?

Family-friendly policies allow workers to meet their family responsibilities, along with their work responsibilities. Family-friendly policies often entail a "flexible workplace," where the workday or workplace can be altered according to the family and caring responsibilities of the worker. This report looks at two types of flexible workplace policies—scheduling flexibility and access to leave for the birth of a child (a form of anticipated leave)—and finds that they have either positive effects or little to no effect on wages.

Workplace flexibility can take the following forms:

- **Scheduling flexibility**. Allows workers to set or alter their day-to-day schedule.

- **Unanticipated leave**. Allows workers to take leave for personal obligations, such as taking care of a sick child or attending a parent-teacher meeting.

- **Anticipated paid leave**. Gives workers time off for vacations, longer-term illnesses, and family caregiving.

- **Work location**. Offers flexibility in the location of work, allowing employees to telecommute.

- **Career flexibility**. Offers workers the chance to move in and out of the labor market, as necessary, to balance their work and family life. . . .

Mothers in the Workplace

Women's earnings are an increasingly important part of total family income. Over the past few decades, mothers' employment rates have risen considerably and their earnings now comprise about two-fifths of family income. As more mothers now remain in the labor market while they have children in the home, new questions have arisen concerning how parents can balance their work responsibilities with the caring needs of their families.

Most workers arrive on the job at times that suit their employer, having little or no say about their schedule. For parents, this can pose difficulties, as they may need to coordinate their work hours with their child's daycare provider or school schedule. Further, most workers do not have access to paid sick leave or other paid leave that would allow them to take time off work when they—or their children—need extra care.

"Family-friendly" policies, in the form of workplace flexibility, can provide parents with the flexibility and time off that they need to balance their work responsibilities with their commitment to their family. Workplace flexibility policies range from reduced hours or flexible schedules to time off to care for a family member.

Taking advantage of workplace flexibility may, however, entail costs such as lower wages or fewer fringe benefits. For example, it is often noted that part-time work, which parents may choose in order to have more family time, results in lower wages compared to other comparably skilled workers. On the other hand, these policies may increase the ability of mothers to remain in the labor market, thus improving their earnings over time compared to those mothers who drop out of the labor force.

Effects on Wages

This report looks at two specific kinds of workplace flexibility—scheduling flexibility and access to leave for the birth of a child (a form of anticipated leave)—and finds that they have either positive effects or little or no effect on mothers' wages. Mothers who worked before the birth of their first child and had access to paid leave for maternity have present-day wages that are 9 percent higher than mothers who had not taken leave, controlling for the mother's personal and job-related characteristics. There was no effect on wages for mothers who self-financed their maternity leave.

Being able to choose a schedule that fits with caring responsibilities does not appear to lower wages. Mothers who reported that they were working a particular schedule because it fit in with their caring responsibilities have wages that are not statistically different from mothers who have no choice about their schedules. Thus, having this kind of flexibility does not entail a price for mothers, once we account for part-time status.

These findings should focus policymakers' attention on what "works" for working parents, and the role that social policy can play in improving labor market outcomes for workers across the wage distribution. If workplace flexibility can help parents by improving their options for work/family balance without creating wage penalties, then policymakers should focus on ways to extend these policies to more workers and to create labor standards that recognize the importance of work/family balance for working families. . . .

Under the Family and Medical Leave Act (FMLA), about half of women in the U.S. labor market currently [as of 2005] have access to unpaid leave for the birth or adoption of a child or to care for a sick family member. However, just over half do not have access. Moving towards universality in access to leave could help to close the gap in women's pay and could help more women stay in the labor market over time.

The Family Gap

Over their lifetimes, women earn less than half of what men earn; over a 15 year period, prime-age women workers earn 38 percent of what men earn. Recent research has pointed to the presence of children and the lack of family-friendly policies as one of the most important factors explaining women's lower lifetime earnings. The "family gap" is the gap among women between those with and without children. As with the gender gap, much of the family gap is explained by workers' demographics, educational attainment, job characteristics, and years of experience. The unexplained portion of the family gap—the gap due to the presence of children—is about 5 percent, some of which may be due to leave-taking or breaks in employment for caring for families.

Family-friendly policies may mitigate the family gap in pay. A cross-country comparison of seven industrialized nations finds that the family gap is largest in the United Kingdom, followed by the other Anglo-American nations and Germany. Parents in Anglo-American nations have less access to family-friendly policies. Researchers point to these differences in maternity and child care policies in creating differences in the family gap across countries.

The returns to having paid maternity leave are high; however, the costs of providing this leave are relatively low. A recent [as of 2005] estimate for the state of Massachusetts found that implementing a paid parental leave program of 12 weeks at 50 percent of wages would incur an annual cost on every worker in the state of between $19 and $22—about the price of two movie tickets. Thus, a small investment up front can lead to significant gains for working mothers over the rest of their careers.

The Government Must Help

One thing is certain: We cannot rely on the private sector to voluntarily provide all workers with workplace flexibility. This analysis finds that most mothers—especially those without any college—did not have pay during maternity leave for the birth of their first child. Workplaces have not created broad paid family leave programs on the heels of the FMLA. We can no longer view the rigidities of the workplace as an individual problem; rather, we must view them as something that poses a threat to all families and is something that must be dealt with by policy.

Flexible Schedules Increasing

According to the Bureau of Labor Statistics, slightly more men than women worked flexible schedules even before the Sept. 11, 2001, terrorist attacks on the World Trade Center and the Pentagon, which made many Americans rethink their approach to life. In May 2001, about 30 percent of men and 27.4 percent of women said they were on some type of flex schedule.

The data include not only people who arrange schedules by choice, but also those who work alternative shifts, including overnight, which may be a contributing factor to the higher percentage of men using flextime in this particular survey. According to the data, men were more likely than women to work alternative shifts, 16.4 percent compared with 12.1 percent.

But as more employees desire a flexible schedule and as technology continues to evolve, with laptops, e-mail, cell phones and pagers only getting better, the fear that employees won't be connected to the office by working from home or at varying hours is slowly disappearing. And as companies become more global, with work taking place at all hours, flexible schedules—from both an employer and employee standpoint—are becoming more necessary.

Meghan Collins Sullivan,
"Flextime Bids Fond Farewell to the 9-to-5,"
Washington Post, *September 5, 2004.*

There is some movement in this direction. In 2002, California governor Gray Davis signed a bill providing workers with paid leave to care for a sick family member or bond with a new child. This legislation, which took effect in June 2004, is the first of its kind in the United States. This law pays workers 55 to 60 percent of wages (subject to a cap) for six weeks of leave and is financed entirely by payroll taxes on employees.

Other states are working towards implementing their own paid leave legislation; such legislation just passed the Senate in Washington State, for example.

Workers need access to workplace flexibility to allow them [to] coordinate their personal lives with their work lives. Employers need government intervention to level the playing field. Employers who offer workplace flexibility should not bear the full costs of implementing good workplace practices, while other employers are allowed to ignore their employees' needs. Nationally applicable labor standards should include workplace flexibility policies, such as access to paid leaves and flexible scheduling. Relying on the goodwill of employers has meant that many workers, especially low-wage workers, do not have access to any kind of flexibility. The solutions to this problem are to be found not only in employer policies, but through broader universal policy solutions as well.

> *"[Single workers] have expressed dismay that they felt they were asked to work more when employees with families needed time away from work."*

Family-Friendly Policies Do Not Help Single Women

Amy Joyce

In the following viewpoint, Amy Joyce, Washington Post *staff writer, argues that unmarried and single women do not benefit from family-friendly policies. Although corporations have done much to help women with children, few have implanted policies that respect the needs of all of their workers. Joyce notes that those companies that offer flexible schedules and other "employee-friendly" policies do so in part because policies that include singles and childless employees can be seen as discriminatory.*

As you read, consider the following questions:

1. By what percentage did the number of single-person households increase between 1970 and 2004?
2. What are some strategies that companies are using to accommodate single employees?

Amy Joyce, "Kid-Friendly Policies Don't Help Singles," *Washington Post*, September 17, 2006. Copyright © 2006 The Washington Post. Reprinted with permission.

3. What is the difference between family-friendly policies and "flexible culture" policies?

If Barbara Rose could, she would love to have three to six months off from her full-time job as a critical-care nurse in San Diego to finish her doctoral dissertation. But since she never had children, and never intends to, she knows she won't get the same sort of leave many of her new-mom co-workers have received.

Her boss did, however, offer her every other Friday off in January, which she took. It was a nice help, she said, but it's not the same leave or benefits available to parents.

She celebrates births and adoptions. She appreciates that her co-workers are producing the next generation of nurses. She knows they need that leave and is glad they have it. But, she asked, "must I have to give birth just to have my time be viewed as of equal value as the time my colleagues spend on their families?"

Single Workers Left Out

Since corporations started paying attention to "family-friendly" benefits in the late 1980s, child-free and single workers have wondered where their benefits were. They have expressed dismay that they felt they were asked to work more when employees with families needed time away from work. Others thought they were given the more difficult jobs with less financial reward because those with children were considered to have greater financial needs.

The proportion of single-person households increased to 26.4 percent in 2003 from 17.1 percent in 1970, according to 2003 census figures. Add to that the number of married couples without children, and that's about 55 percent of U.S. households.

Unmarried America, formerly the American Association for Single People, says about 40 percent of the workforce is made up of unmarried people, many of whom don't need leave to take care of children or a sick spouse. So many of them wonder: What about me?

The Family and Medical Leave Act allows anyone who is working for an organization of 50 or more employees to take time off for a serious health condition. It also allows employees to take time off to care for a sick "immediate" family member, defined as spouse, child or parent. But some workers with no children might define an immediate family differently.

Childless workers thought they worked more than people who were married with kids and that they had to work holidays more often and did not have access to as many benefits, according to "Beyond Family-Friendly: Singles-Friendly Work Cultures and Employee Attachment." The lead author of the study is Wendy Casper, an assistant professor of management at the University of Texas at Arlington who got her master's and PhD at George Mason University.

Casper began to study the impact of family-friendly workplaces after she was traveling as a consultant and realized that the other consultants who traveled were all single with no children—as she was, and is. "It started occurring to me: What about those people who can't use these benefits? How do they feel about it?" she said. "People do have different needs." And it's a business imperative to try to make things as equal as possible. "If you have a good workforce that people are happy to be in and their needs are being recognized, they are willing to do things that aren't part of their job just to help the company."

Accomodating Singles

Some companies are working to accommodate singles.

For instance, Dickstein Shapiro LLP does not limit an alternative-schedule policy to people who want it for child-rearing reasons, said Michael Nannes, managing partner. "We can't discriminate based on lifestyle."

Work/Life Balance Strategies for Single Workers

If you're single and wish your employer was a bit more tuned in to your needs, here are some things you can do:

- **Take stock.** First, feel free to increase the balance in your life . . . Rather than feeling guilty about wanting more balance, look at the specific goal you're trying to achieve. . . .

- **Understand the downside.** If you're looking for increased flexibility at work, make sure your career expectations are realistic . . . You may not advance at the same pace you would if you put in 24/7 at the office. Make sure you're okay with the tradeoffs.

- **Ask.** After you know specifically what you want, ask for it. But be strategic. . . . Articulate your goal for balance, your job responsibilities and how you'll make sure your work gets done. And don't worry about telling your boss exactly what you'll be doing. He or she doesn't need to know you're heading to a Pilates class. . . .

- **Do your homework.** If you feel like your boss takes advantage of your singleness, examine your company's workplace policies. Is "marital status" listed in its nondiscrimination policy? . . . Are employee assistance programs equitable to both single and married employees? . . . Then approach your employer with your findings.

- **Form networks.** Many companies have support groups for gay and lesbian employees or for employees who are parents. Ask if you can form a support group for single workers. . . .

- **Find help.** Identify allies in your company who can help you effect change. If, however, you feel like you're bumping your head against the proverbial wall, look to enlist the support of a national organization such as Unmarried America . . .

Susan Bowles, "Single Workers Need Work/life Balance, Too!"
www.unmarriedamerica.org, 2006.

At least six years ago, Maria Colsey Heard was an associate at Dickstein. Married with no children, she decided to try an alternative schedule so she could have her Fridays off. Those days were used for errands: veterinarian, dry cleaner, dentist. "Like everyone else who works full time, I found it difficult to balance work duties and home responsibilities," she said.

She went on the schedule when she was still an associate. "A few people told me I was crazy and would not be able to advance if I did this," she said. But Heard, a litigator, is now a partner. She is also a new mother. When she returns to work, she will return to her four-day-a-week schedule. "But my priorities for my Fridays will change."

"My philosophy from the beginning was that you really want to be balanced in what you do," said Pandit Wright, senior executive vice president of human resources at Discovery Communications Inc., who noted she is a single-no-kids.

She attended a meeting on her first day 11 years ago where several parents said they wanted on-site child care. But there were few people with children then, she said. And she was more interested in building a culture that "was not just family-friendly." She said, "We wanted a flexible culture."

The first thing she did was give three personal days off a year for anyone. That's on top of a minimum of 10 days of vacation leave and 10 days of sick leave. The company calls the personal days "balance days."

Employee-Friendly Policies

Michael Hunston, manager of administration at Discovery, uses those days to volunteer with an organization in the District. He also benefits from Discovery's health-care coverage for domestic partners. When his partner was moving between jobs, Hunston was able to cover both of them. "I never even thought of the benefits package at Discovery being family-friendly or not family-friendly—just employee-friendly."

Other services, such as a concierge for people to get dry cleaning done on site, a wellness center, and flex-time and telework options are available to everyone on a case-by-case basis, Wright added.

But, Wright said, some things are available to parents that aren't available to those who don't have children. "I don't believe a person should think in terms of tit for tat," she said. "Like it or not, the next generation is someone you're going to have to deal with. It behooves all of us to have an environment where parents can do what they do."

There is still no on-site day care center at Discovery, but Wright said the company is looking into having a site near the headquarters. At the same time, the company is looking into a sabbatical program for all of its employees.

The fact that she is single with no kids "helped to always keep in mind you didn't want the backlash," she said. "I didn't want to be the person who just has things for people with kids."

Periodical Bibliography

The following articles have been selected to supplement the diverse views presented in this chapter.

Catherine Albiston	"Anti-Essentialism and the Work/Family Dilemma," *Berkeley Journal of Gender, Law & Justice*, 2005.
Lisa Belkin	"Charting a Path from Bed to Desk," *New York Times*, January 28, 2007.
Mariah Boone	"Incomplete Revolution," *Off Our Backs*, March 2006.
Hillary Chura	"Some Signs of Easier Re-entry after Breaks to Rear Children," *New York Times*, November 11, 2005.
CQ Researcher	"Future of Feminism," April 14, 2006.
Machine Design	"Why Money Doesn't Bring Happiness," September 14, 2006.
Mary A. Naylor	"There's No Workforce like Home," *Business Week Online*, May 2, 2006.
Ellen K. Scott, Andrew S. London, and Allison Hurst	"Instability in Patchworks of Child Care when Moving from Welfare to Work," *Journal of Marriage & Family*, May 2005.
Jennifer Swanberg, Caroline Macke, and T.K. Logan	"Working Women Making It Work," *Journal of Interpersonal Violence*, March 2007.
Stephen Sweet and Phyllis Moen	"Integrating Educational Careers in Work and Family," *Community, Work, and Family*, May 2007.
Diane Weathers	"Is Your 9-to-5 a 24/7?" *Essence*, March 2004.
Peter C. Winwood, Antony Winefield, and Kurt Lushington	"Work-Related Fatigue and Recovery: The Contribution of Age, Domestic Responsibilities, and Shiftwork," *Journal of Advanced Nursing*, November 2006.

CHAPTER 4

Are Working Women Good for Families?

Chapter Preface

For much of the twentieth century, women were sent the message that they must choose between having a family and having a career. They were told that the time commitments required to be successful in any line of work exclude the possibility of starting and raising a family until well after the time when women's bodies are capable of doing so. Such assertions, established in society and in the workplace, left many women feeling hopeless and fearful that they might make the wrong decision. Fortunately, attitudes about the subject are changing, though quite slowly, and many women have realized that it is possible to have both. Now the conflict seems to focus on when. At what point in her career should a woman have a baby?

Many critics have noted that the usual career path follows a man's life cycle. He must work very hard at the beginning and all the way through his early twenties and well into his thirties before he is finally established in his career. Unfortunately, those same years mark women's fertile period. Studies have shown that after age thirty-five, women's chances of conceiving decrease dramatically. According to a 2003 study in *British Medical Journal*, the conception rate for women aged 35–39 is 60% after one year of trying and 85% at two years of trying. In addition, birth defect rates begin to climb after age 35.

Although many media reports released during the 1980s and 1990s announcing the lack of time left on the "biological clocks" of career women were certainly frightening to women who had waited to start their families, many subsequent reports focused on the realities of waiting past a certain age. Rather than scaring women into thinking they are running out of time to become mothers, many writers began arguing that the important goal is to educate women about their bodies. According to Pamela Madeson, executive director of the American Infertility Association, "Those women who are at the top of their game could have had it all, children and career, if they wanted it. The problem was, nobody told them the truth about their bodies." Women who are educated about their fertility can make better decisions.

Part of the problem, argues Nancy Gibbs in "Making Time for a Baby," is that "Childlessness is a private sorrow; the miracle baby is an inevitable headline." In other words, few women openly talk about their failed attempts at getting pregnant, while the few women who are out of the normal range of childbearing years who manage to get pregnant make the news, which gives women false hope that they can wait until they are ready to have children. While many fertility treatments exist, there are limits to such technologies.

Women who feel that they cannot or have no desire to stop their careers to have children have options that might improve their chances of conceiving later in life. For example, some women choose to freeze their eggs, because one of the problems with conceiving past forty is chromosomally damaged eggs. Freezing eggs while they are young reduces the possibilities of such damage.

Of course, what all of these issues demonstrate is that there is no one right time for a career woman to start her family. She must weigh her options and educate herself about her body. Like other issues debated in this chapter, deciding if and when to have a baby is an issue that is much debated.

| "*Professional women are more likely to get divorced, more likely to cheat and less likely to have children.*"

Career Women Make Bad Wives

Michael Noer

In the following viewpoint, Michael Noer, executive news editor for Forbes.com, argues that men should not marry career women because the marriage will likely end in divorce. He asserts that professional women are more likely to get divorced, more likely to cheat on their spouses, and less likely to have children. Noer notes that when both spouses work outside the home, there is little time left for necessary household chores, which leads to marital discord.

As you read, consider the following questions:

1. How does the author define "career girl"?

2. How many more times are spouses with graduate degrees likely to cheat than spouses with high school diplomas?

3. Individual net worth drops by an average of what percentage following a divorce?

Guys: a word of advice. Marry pretty women or ugly ones. Short ones or tall ones. Blondes or brunettes. Just, whatever you do, don't marry a woman with a career.

Rocky Marriages

Why? Because if many social scientists are to be believed, you run a higher risk of having a rocky marriage. While everyone knows that marriage can be stressful, recent studies [as of 2006] have found professional women are more likely to get divorced, more likely to cheat and less likely to have children. And if they do have kids, they are more likely to be unhappy about it. A recent study in *Social Forces*, a research journal, found that women—even those with a "feminist" outlook— are happier when their husband is the primary breadwinner.

Not a happy conclusion, especially given that many men, particularly successful men, are attracted to women with similar goals and aspirations. And why not? After all, your typical career girl is well educated, ambitious, informed and engaged. All seemingly good things, right? Sure . . . at least until you get married. Then, to put it bluntly, the more successful she is, the more likely she is to grow dissatisfied with you. Sound familiar?

Many factors contribute to a stable marriage, including the marital status of your spouse's parents (folks with divorced parents are significantly more likely to get divorced themselves), age at first marriage, race, religious beliefs and socio-economic status. And, of course, many working women are indeed happily and fruitfully married—it's just that they are less likely to be so than nonworking women. And that, statistically speaking, is the rub.

To be clear, we're not talking about a high school dropout minding a cash register. For our purposes, a "career girl" has a university-level (or higher) education, works more than 35 hours a week outside the home and makes more than $30,000 a year.

Rights and Responsibilities Go Hand-in-Hand

For the last 30 years, discussions about women in the workforce have been guided by the unspoken rule, "Men's Opinions Don't Count."

But then women's one-sided conversations lapsed into over-wrought declamations about men who didn't pitch in around the house, forgetting that men often put in longer hours on the job, commute longer distances, and do physical labor that leaves them exhausted.

Doesn't mowing the grass, killing creepy-crawlers that traipse through the kitchen, clearing leaves out of the gutter, and coaching Little League count for anything?

And let's not forget the old axiom that rights and responsibilities go hand-in-hand. If women are demanding more rights, then what additional duties—like compulsory registration for the draft—are they going to shoulder?

Carey Roberts, "Don't Marry a Career Woman:
The Debate Heats Up," www.newswithviews.com,
September 16, 2006, www.newswithviews.com/Roberts/carey134.htm.

If a host of studies are to be believed, marrying these women is asking for trouble. If they quit their jobs and stay home with the kids, they will be unhappy (*Journal of Marriage and Family*, 2003). They will be unhappy if they make more money than you do (*Social Forces*, 2006). You will be unhappy if they make more money than you do (*Journal of Marriage and Family*, 2001). You will be more likely to fall ill (*American Journal of Sociology*). Even your house will be dirtier (*Institute for Social Research*).

Sharing Work

Why? Well, despite the fact that the link between work, women and divorce rates is complex and controversial, much of the reasoning is based on a lot of economic theory and a bit of common sense. In classic economics, a marriage is, at least in part, an exercise in labor specialization. Traditionally, men have tended to do "market" or paid work outside the home, and women have tended to do "nonmarket" or household work, including raising children. All of the work must get done by somebody, and this pairing, regardless of who is in the home and who is outside the home, accomplishes that goal. Nobel laureate Gary S. Becker argued that when the labor specialization in a marriage decreases—if, for example, both spouses have careers—the overall value of the marriage is lower for both partners because less of the total needed work is getting done, making life harder for both partners and divorce more likely. And, indeed, empirical studies have concluded just that.

In 2004, John H. Johnson examined data from the Survey of Income and Program Participation and concluded that gender has a significant influence on the relationship between work hours and increases in the probability of divorce. Women's work hours consistently increase divorce, whereas increases in men's work hours often have no statistical effect. "I also find that the incidence in divorce is far higher in couples where both spouses are working than in couples where only one spouse is employed," Johnson says. A few other studies, which have focused on employment (as opposed to working hours), have concluded that working outside the home actually increases marital stability, at least when the marriage is a happy one. But even in these studies, wives' employment does correlate positively to divorce rates, when the marriage is of "low marital quality."

Extramarital Affairs

The other reason a career can hurt a marriage will be obvious to anyone who has seen his or her mate run off with a co-worker: When your spouse works outside the home, chances increase that he or she will meet someone more likable than you. "The work environment provides a host of potential partners," researcher Adrian J. Blow reported in *The Journal of Marital and Family Therapy*, "and individuals frequently find themselves spending a great deal of time with these individuals."

There's more: According to a wide-ranging review of the published literature, highly educated people are more likely to have had extramarital sex (those with graduate degrees are 1.75 times more likely to have cheated than those with high school diplomas). Additionally, individuals who earn more than $30,000 a year are more likely to cheat.

And if the cheating leads to divorce, you're really in trouble. Divorce has been positively correlated with higher rates of alcoholism, clinical depression and suicide. Other studies have associated divorce with increased rates of cancer, stroke, and sexually transmitted disease. Plus, divorce is financially devastating. According to one recent study [as of 2006] on "Marriage and Divorce's Impact on Wealth," published in *The Journal of Sociology*, divorced people see their overall net worth drop an average of 77%.

Reasons to Marry

So why not just stay single? Because, academically speaking, a solid marriage has a host of benefits beyond just individual "happiness." There are broader social and health implications as well. According to a 2004 paper titled "What Do Social Scientists Know about the Benefits of Marriage?" marriage is positively associated with "better outcomes for children under most circumstances" and higher earnings for adult men, and "being married and being in a satisfying marriage are positively associated with health and negatively associated with mortality." In other words, a good marriage is associated with a higher income, a longer, healthier life and better-adjusted kids.

A word of caution, though: As with any social scientific study, it's important not to confuse correlation with causation. In other words, just because married folks are healthier than single people, it doesn't mean that marriage is causing the health gains. It could just be that healthier people are more likely to be married.

| *"Wives' full-time employment is now associated with increased marital stability."*

Career Women Do Not Make Bad Wives

Stephanie Coontz

Stephanie Coontz is a history professor at Evergreen State College in Olympia, Washington, and director of research and public education at the Council on Contemporary Families. In the following viewpoint, she argues that highly educated and career-oriented women are not more likely to be unhappy in marriages. Coontz counters previous assumptions about the probability that professional women will marry with current studies. She found that as cultural expectations of gender roles have changed, so have the assumptions that men have about who makes a good lifelong partner.

As you read, consider the following questions:

1. What was the median age of marriage for women in 1960? In 2007?

2. According to Heather Boushey's research, what percentage of women aged 30-44 who earned more than $100,000 a year are married?

Stephanie Coontz, "The Romantic Life of Brainiacs," *The Boston Globe*, February 18, 2007. Reproduced by permission of the author.

3. According to Rosalind Barnett and Caryl Rivers,
   what percentage of college-educated women make
   more than their husbands?

Pity the overschooled old maid and the lonely career
woman. Highly educated or high-achieving women are
less likely to marry and have children than other women. If
they do marry, they are more likely to divorce. Even if they
don't divorce, their marriages will be less happy. And, oh, yes,
they'll be sexually frustrated, too. . . .

But are these women really educating themselves out of
the marriage market? If a woman reads Proust or computes
calculus, is she unable to attract a mate?

Conventional wisdom says the answer to both questions is
yes. But a close look at the historical transformation of marriage in America suggests that educated women now have a
surprising advantage when it comes to matrimony. . . .

Old Attitudes

The myth of the bitter, sexually unsatisfied female college
graduate has never been true. Surveys from the 1890s to the
present reveal that college-educated women have always been
at least as satisfied with their emotional and sexual lives as
their less-educated counterparts. But until recently, it was true
that women who completed the highest levels of education or
landed high-status, high-paying jobs were less likely than
other women to marry and have children. They were often
perfectly happy with their choices, but the fact remains that
many women did have to choose between family life and
achievement in the public sphere.

One reason for this was that men of the past were more
interested in marrying someone who would cook or clean for
them than in an intellectual equal. In 2001, University of
Texas psychologist David M. Buss and colleagues compared
mate preferences based on national surveys taken for several

decades beginning in 1939. Their research, published in the *Journal of Marriage and Family*, found that in 1956, education and intelligence ranked 11th among the things men desired in a mate. The respondents were more attracted to someone who was a good cook and housekeeper, had a pleasing disposition, and was refined and neat. By 1967, education and intelligence had moved up only one place, to number 10, and still counted for less than being a good cook or displaying neatness and refinement.

Another reason for the lower marriage rates of educated women was the fact, still true today, that women tend to postpone marriage while they acquire higher education or establish themselves in a career. And back in the 1950s, a marriage postponed was often a marriage forgone. In 1960, the median age of marriage for women was just 20. Half of all women married before they left their teens, and a woman who was still single at the ripe old age of 24 had much less chance of ever marrying than a single woman that age today. She was what the Japanese called "Christmas Cake," unlikely to find a buyer after the 25th. If she had a graduate degree, her chances of marriage were particularly slim. As late as the 1980s, women with PhDs or the equivalent were significantly less likely to marry than women with high school degrees.

But all this has changed in the past 25 years [between 1980 and 2005]. For one thing, the age at which people marry has risen considerably. The median age for a first marriage nationally is now 25.5 for women and 27 for men. It is even higher for those with graduate degrees. In Massachusetts, the median age at first marriage is 27.2 for women and 29.2 for men. The state's high proportion of never-married individuals (the country's third highest) primarily reflects the fact that Massachusetts residents marry at an older age—not that they will never marry.

Better Chances of Marriage

In fact, educated women nationwide now have a better chance of marrying, especially at an older age, than other women. In a historic reversal of past trends—one that is good news for young girls who like to use big words—college graduates and high-earning women are now more likely to marry than women with less education and lower earnings, although they are older when they do so. Even women with PhDs no longer face a "success penalty" in their nuptial prospects. It might feel that way in their 20s, when women with advanced degrees marry at a lower rate than other women the same age. But by their 30s, women with advanced degrees catch up, marrying at a higher rate than their same-aged counterparts with less education.

The same holds for high-earning women. Economist Heather Boushey of the Center for Economic and Policy Research in Washington, D.C., found that women between the ages of 28 and 35 who work full time and earn more than $55,000 a year or who have a graduate or professional degree are just as likely to be married as other working women of the same age. And among women aged 30 to 44 who earn more than $100,000 a year, 88 percent are married, compared with 82 percent of other women in the same age range.

Despite the many scare stories aimed at educated black women, this is one area in which the usual double jeopardy of being black and female does not apply. True, educated black women are less likely to marry than their white counterparts, reflecting the fact that marriage rates among African-Americans are, in general, lower than marriage rates of whites. But having an advanced degree is not an additional impediment to a black woman's chance of marriage. In fact, says economist Elaina Rose of the University of Washington in Seattle, there is now a "success premium" for highly educated black women, who are more likely to get married and also more likely to stay married than other black women. Fewer

Marriage Rates Rise for Educated Women

The tradeoff that women make between education and marriage seems to be going the way of the horse and carriage.

As recently as 1980, the more years of post-high school education a woman had, the less likely she was to marry.

Elaina Rose, an economist at the University of Washington, termed this tradeoff the success gap. But after examining the 1980, 1990 and 2000 Census, Rose has determined that while the success gap still exists, it is narrowing fast.

In 1980, a woman with three years of graduate school was 13 percent less likely to be married than a woman with only a high-school diploma. By 2000, that gap shrank to less than 5 percent, according to Rose, who presented her findings at a conference in Boston last week.

"If we extrapolate this forward, the gap won't be here in 2010," says Rose. "The tradeoff between education and family is just not there the way it was before. It's disappearing."

Kelly DiNardo, "Marriage Rates Rise for Educated Women," Women's E-News, www.womensenews.org/article.cfm/dyn/aid/1777, April 6, 2004.

than 50 percent of African-American women with a high school education are married, compared with more than 55 percent of African-American women with 19 years of school.

All women with PhDs are still slightly less likely to have children than other women, but the difference has been shrinking rapidly. And high-achieving women in general are as likely as other married working women to have children, although, again, they often do so at an older age.

Changing Expectations

One reason educated women are more likely to marry today than in the past is that modern men are less threatened by equality and more interested in finding a mate who can share the burdens of breadwinning. Many studies show that men now want a wife who is at a similar educational or occupational level. The 2001 *Journal of Marriage and Family* paper found that in mate-preference surveys taken in 1985 and 1996, intelligence and education had moved up to number 5 on men's list of desirable qualities in a mate in both surveys, ahead of good looks. Meanwhile, the desire for a good cook and housekeeper had dropped to 14th place in both surveys, near the bottom of the 18-point scale. And in choosing a spouse, males with a college degree rate good looks much lower in importance than do high school graduates. "In a high-achieving man's definition of an A-list woman, the A increasingly stands for 'accomplished,'" says Deborah Siegel, former director of special projects at the National Council for Research on Women, in New York, and coauthor of the forthcoming book *Sisterhood, Interrupted: From Radical Women to Grrls Gone Wild* [published in 2007].

Furthermore, college-educated couples have lower divorce rates than any other educational group. And in the last 30 years, while the marriages of less-educated women became less stable, the marriages of college-educated women became more stable. College graduates are more likely to have egalitarian ideas about sharing housework and breadwinning, and recent [as of 2007] research shows that egalitarian ideas and behaviors improve marital satisfaction for both men and women.

Highly educated women are more likely to work outside the home than less-educated women, even after they become mothers. In the past, employed wives tended to divorce at higher rates than non-employed wives, not because working harmed the marriage, but because women who worked had more options to leave a bad marriage. But [in 2006], a study discovered that wives' full-time employment is now associated with increased marital stability.

Sharing the Workload

So the doomsayers are wrong. Educated men and women are more likely to marry and less likely to divorce than others. And guess what? They have better sex lives, too. According to sociologist Virginia Rutter of Framingham State College, surveys show that educated couples engage in more variety in their sex lives. They are, for example, more likely to participate in oral sex, and educated women are more likely to receive oral sex as well as perform it. "Education breaks down gender taboos that can be at the heart of a lot of sexual disappointments," notes Rutter, "and education helps men in particular to loosen up sexually." Educated husbands are also more likely to help with housework, which turns out to be a potent aphrodisiac.

Psychologist John Gottman, professor emeritus at the University of Washington in Seattle, found that when men do more housework, their wives are more likely to be "in the mood" for sex. . . .

Psychologist Rosalind Barnett of Brandeis University and journalism professor Caryl Rivers of Boston University have found that 42 percent of college-educated married women who work outearn their partners, and their marriages are just as stable as those in which the husband makes more than his wife. In fact, Barnett's new study of dual-earner couples, based on data from the 1990s, found that as the wife worked more, the husband's view of the quality of his marriage actually improved. Surveys also show that the longer a woman holds a job, the more child care and housework her husband is likely to do, and that well-educated men have increased their housework more than less-educated ones.

How about the suggestion that women tamp down their expectations and create a "family myth" of fairness? That's one way to achieve family harmony. But another way is for men to actually do their fair share at home. Studies have shown that men whose attitudes become more egalitarian during their marriage report higher marital satisfaction, and so do their wives; they also have better sex lives and more socially aware children. Among couples with both partners in the work-force—the majority today—men and women who adopt less egalitarian ideas over the years become more psychologically anxious and depressed than their more progressive peers, according to an analysis of dual-earner couples conducted by Jacquelyn B. James, director of research for the Boston College Center for Work & Family.

It's true that when men don't live up to women's expectations of fairness, contemporary wives often become unhappy. And, as my mom's favorite T-shirt put it, "If mamma ain't happy, ain't nobody happy." But one of the biggest predictors that a marriage will be stable and happy, according to Gott-man, the psychologist, is if a husband responds positively when his wife expresses a desire for change. It helps if she asks nicely. But it doesn't help if she avoids the issue and lets her discontent simmer.

Modern couples have more to negotiate than couples in the past, and that sometimes leads to conflict. But healthy conflict is often the way to marital growth. And besides, there's always make-up sex—at which college-educated couples no doubt excel.

"Many of the gains of professional-class working women have been leveraged on the backs of poor women."

Working Mothers Are Exploiting Hired Care Givers

Caitlin Flanagan

Caitlin Flanagan is an award-winning freelance writer and author of To Hell with All That. *In the following viewpoint, she argues that professional-class women exploit underclass women who care for their children. Rather than helping these women, who often come from all over the world seeking safety and a better life in the United States, career women pay them little and continue to degrade the work that they do for them. Ultimately, Flanagan asserts that professional-class women must work together to lift poor women and children out of poverty even if it might mean inconveniencing their own lives.*

As you read, consider the following questions:

1. According to the author, from what two areas of the world are American nannies recruited?

Caitlin Flanagan, "How Serfdom Saved the Women's Movement: Dispatches from the Nanny Wars," as first published in *The Atlantic Monthly*, vol. 293, March 2004, pp. 113–14, 126–28. Copyright © 2004 by Caitlin Flanagan. Reprinted by permission of William Morris Agency, LLC on behalf of the author.

2. According to the author, why do most upper-middle-class women hire nannies?

3. According to the *Girlfriends' Guide* series, how do most Americans find their nannies?

With the arrival of a cheap, easily exploited army of poor and luckless women—fleeing famine, war, the worst kind of poverty, leaving behind their children to do it, facing the possibility of rape or death on the expensive and secret journey—one of the noblest tenets of second-wave feminism collapsed like a house of cards. The new immigrants were met at the docks not by a highly organized and politically power-ful group of American women intent on bettering the lot of their sex but, rather, by an equally large army of educated professional-class women with booming careers who needed their children looked after and their houses cleaned. Any sup-posed equivocations about the moral justness of white women's employing dark-skinned women to do their [grunt] work simply evaporated.

The process by which the First World has been flooded with immigrant female domestic workers during the past two decades [in the 1980s and 1990s] (in such overwhelming num-bers that researchers are now remarking on the "feminization of migration") is fairly well documented, considering that so much of it is done in secret. There are several established trade routes along which future nannies are transported, the most desperate of which takes women from Southeast Asia to Middle Eastern countries such as Kuwait and Saudi Arabia, destinations so notorious for the mistreatment of domestic workers that I am put in mind of Winston Churchill's old say-ing: "When you're going through hell, keep going." For Ameri-cans the two mother lodes of nannies are Central America and the Caribbean. . . .

How these workers became available to middle-class women is well known and amply reported, both in the press and in dozens of fine books, including Rhacel Salazar Parreñas's *Servants of Globalization* and Grace Chang's *Disposable Domestics*. But how so many middle-class American women went from not wanting to oppress other women to viewing that oppression as a central part of their own liberation—that is a complicated and sorry story. In it you will find the seeds of things we don't like to discuss much, including the elitism and hypocrisy of the contemporary feminist movement, the tendency of working and nonworking mothers to pit themselves against one another, and the way that adult middle-class life has become so intensely, laughably child-centered that in the past month I have chaperoned my children to eight birthday parties, yet not attended a single cocktail party (do they even exist anymore?). . . .

Choosing to Use Nannies

So here we have the crux of the problem: ask an upper-middle-class woman why she is exploiting another woman for child care, and she will cry that she has to do it because there's no universal day care. But get a bunch of professional-class mothers together, and they will freely admit that day care sucks; get a nanny. This was a truth that Naomi Wolf—feminist, Yalie, Rhodes scholar, big thinker—learned the hard way after giving birth to her first child. In *Misconceptions*, Wolf reports,

> I never thought I would become one of those women who took up a foreordained place in a hierarchy of class and gender. Yet here we were, to my horror and complicity, shaping our new family structure along class and gender lines— daddy at work, mommy and caregiver from two different economic classes, sharing the baby work during the day.

Her dreams of parenthood, apparently formed while tripping across green New Haven quadrangles on her way to feminist-theory classes, were starkly different: "I had wanted us to be a mother and a father raising children side by side, the man moving into the world of children, the woman into the world of work, in equitable balance, maybe each working flexibly from home, the two making the same world and sharing the same experiences and values." She had wanted a revolution; what she got was a Venezuelan.

I am about the same age as Naomi Wolf, and we had children at about the same time, but I had neither expected nor wanted a revolution. I did not have a single dream about moving into the world of work when I was a girl. In fact, when I concluded that being a girl was in every way superior to being a boy, my two top pieces of evidence—freely offered, never challenged—consisted of the facts that I would never have to go either to Vietnam or to a job. . . .

What I dreamed about was getting married and having babies and running a household. I did, as a young woman, teach school, but I always thought of it as an engaging time killer until the babies arrived. And arrive they did, trailing the advertised clouds of glory, but also (this had not entered into any of my dreams) trailing an awful lot of [grunt] work— [grunt] work that grew more onerous and complicated with each passing month. Furthermore, the [grunt] work seemed to be devolving almost entirely to me, for like Naomi, I had taken up a preordained place in the hierarchy of class and gender.

Finding a Nanny

Don't get me wrong: I got a real kick out of the babies. But the cleaning was putting me in a funk—a bad kind of funk. A feminist-type, really cheesed-off kind of funk. I had expected, merely upon the simple fact of giving birth, to be magically transformed from the kind of woman who likes to spend most of the morning lying on the couch reading and drinking coffee and talking on the telephone to the kind of woman who likes to spend most of the morning tidying up and thinking about what to cook for dinner and inviting other mothers over for a nice chat. It didn't happen. Play dates—a sort of minimum-security lockdown spent in the company of other mildly depressed women and their tiresome, demanding babies—brought on a small death of the spirit, the effects of which I feared might be cumulative. I also felt resentful and sometimes even furious about almost any domestic task that presented itself: why was I supposed to endlessly wipe down the kitchen counters and lug bags of garbage out to the cans and set out the little plastic plates of steamed carrots and mashed bananas that the children touched only in order to hurl them onto the floor? Hadn't every essay I'd ever submitted in college come back with a little mash note telling me I was in some way special, a cut above, meant for something? Wasn't I designed for more important things than putting away Lego blocks and loading the dishwasher? I was! It was time, *Cherchez la femme.*

How did I find her? It was easy. The city is full of them. If you want to find a contractor who will remodel your kitchen sometime before the next presidential election without disappearing for weeks on end midway through the job or cracking the unsealed Italian marble you special-ordered from a catalogue, good luck to you. But if you want someone to take charge of your children, you can take your pick, and they can all start tomorrow. As Vicki Iovine, the author of the *Girlfriends' Guide* series (a collection of books about motherhood that I read so obsessively as a new parent that if every extant copy were destroyed, I could re-create her entire oeuvre in a week), reports, "Most of us find our nannies and sitters through the Girlfriends' Grapevine. We mention to a Girlfriend's nanny that we need help, and she sends one of her friends to us." It has ever been thus. The most engaging work of social history I have ever read is Jonathan Gathorne-Hardy's *The Rise and Fall of the British Nanny.* Describing the hiring process in Victorian England, he reports that so many women were eager for such work that finding a nanny was simple: "When everyone you knew had one, or generally more than one, you obtained your Nanny from a friend or relation who no longer had need of her." In the American segregated South nannies (called "mammies" or, more commonly, "maids") were passed among the members of an extended family with a casualness surely born of slaveholding traditions. Susan Tucker's *Telling Memories Among Southern Women* (another excellent and highly readable book) includes an elderly black woman's account of her experience working as a domestic for a white family in Depression-era Mobile [Alabama]: "They had two children, and one, that little old spoiled Clara, she was a teenager then. I still see her. She used to always get me about working for her, says, 'You raised me, and I want you to raise my daughters.'" During the Great Migration it was common for black women to find domestic work with members of an employer's family who had moved north.

Interesting facts, all of them, but the most striking comment comes from little old spoiled Clara. "You raised me," she said to her former nanny; "I want you to raise my daughters." If there is a single difference between these nanny times and previous ones, it has to do with the intense anxiety working mothers feel about who, exactly, is "raising" their children. I know many women whose children are cared for almost around the clock by nannies, but those women would never be as honest about the fact as Clara. For that reason, and for a hundred others, the subject of nannies is a minefield. For many professional-class women like me, the relationship they have with their children's nanny is a source of the deepest and most painful kind of self-examination. The relationship is in many ways more intense—more vexing, more rewarding, more vital, more fraught—than a marriage. The precise intersection of many women's most passionate impulses—their profound, almost physical love for their children and their ardent wish to make something of themselves beyond their own doorstep—is the exact spot where nannies show up for work each

Nanny Wages and Expectations

In 2000, the U.S. Department of Labor reported that three million mothers leave their children in the care of a nanny or other individual while they work outside the home. The nannies' level of training and education varies widely: some have college degrees in child development while others have only the experience they have acquired over years of caring for children. Their pay varies as well. At the bottom end of the pay scale are nannies earning less than minimum wage, and at the high end are those earning $15 an hour or more. Nannies for the very wealthy command as much as $1,500 a week, with perks such as a separate dwelling with all expenses paid, cell phone, use of a car, health benefits, gym membership, paid vacations, and more.

For a great many nannies, especially live-ins, exploitation in the form of unpaid overtime is common. Most of the nannies' problems stem from the informal, unregulated nature of the work. "She's just like a member of the family" often translates into the nanny being taken advantage of as if she were an indulgent aunt—or Cinderella. Nannies report not getting reimbursed for children's toys, food, or treats; not being paid for gasoline on work-related trips; not being paid if the family goes on vacation; not being paid on time; and having parents reduce their hours at will, changing them every week.

Lynette Padwa,
"How to Get What You Want from the Nanny,"
FamilyEducation.com, 2005.

day. There isn't a nanny in the world who has not received a measure of love that a child would rather have bestowed on his mother. The women's magazines—which have shrewdly staked out as their turf the inexhaustible guilt and anxiety of the working mother—will have none of this. Article after article insists that no one can ever replace a mother, and that a child's love for his mother is unequaled by his feelings for anyone else. Rubbish. To con oneself into thinking that the person who provides daily physical care to a child is not the one he is going to love in a singular and primal way,—a way obviously designed by nature herself to cleave child to mother and vice versa—is to ignore one of the most fundamental truths of childhood. Just as women, often despite their fervent desires to the contrary, tend to fall in love with the men they sleep with, so do small children develop an immediate and consuming passion for the person who feeds and rocks and bathes them every day. It's in the nature of the way they experience love. I have often thought that the American preoccupation with rooting out cruel and unfeeling nannies—buying video cameras sewn into teddy bears, doubling back to the house to peer into windows, and so on—is really a somewhat hysterical reaction to the possibility of the opposite: nannies who share pure and wholly reciprocated love with their charges. This is dangerous territory for all concerned. Is it any wonder that so many nanny jobs end in blowups and abrupt sackings? On the other hand, if you are called out of town for a day or two (as I was for both of my parents' deaths, and— only once, but how thrilling! how important I felt!—for work), is there any more blessed, calming sensation than knowing that your child will be in the hands of someone who knows him and loves him almost as much as you do?

Despair in Separation

What few will admit—because it is painful, because it reveals the unpleasant truth that life presents a series of choices, each of which precludes a host of other attractive possibilities—is that when a mother works, something is lost. Children crave their mothers. They always have and they always will. And women fortunate enough to live in a society where they have access to that greatest of levelers, education, will always have the burning dream of doing something more exciting and important than tidying Lego blocks and running loads of laundry. If you want to make an upper-middle-class woman squeal in indignation, tell her she can't have something. If she works she can't have as deep and connected a relationship with her child as she would if she stayed home and raised him. She can't have the glamour and respect conferred on career women if she chooses instead to spend her days at "Mommy and Me" classes. She can't have both things. I have read numerous accounts of the anguish women have felt leaving small babies with caregivers so that they could go to work, and I don't discount those stories for a moment. That the separation of a woman from her child produces agony for both is one of the most enduring and impressive features of the human experience, and it probably accounts for why we've made it as far as we have. I've read just as many accounts of the despair that descends on some women when their world is abruptly narrowed to the tedium and exhaustion of the nursery; neither do I discount these stories: I've felt that self-same despair.

In my case, the despair was lessened—greatly—by a nanny. Without her I could never have launched a second career as a writer. Her kindness, her patience, and her many (and oftentimes extreme) acts of generosity have shaped my family as much as any other force. But the implications of this solution to my domestic problems are grave, and ever since I read *Doméstica*, two years ago, I have been turning over in my mind the high moral cost of my decision. Even if one pays a fair wage, hires a legal resident of the United States, and pays both one's own share of the required taxes and the employee's, so as not to short her take-home pay (all of which I do), one is still part of a system that exposes women to the brutalities of illegal immigration, only to reward their suffering with the jobs that ease our already comfortable lives.

Improving Working Conditions

It's easy enough to dismiss the dilemma of the professional-class working mother as the whining of the elite. But people

183

are entitled to their lives, and within the context of privilege there are certainly hard choices, disappointments, sorrows. Upper-middle class working mothers may never have calm hearts regarding their choices about work and motherhood, but there are certain things they can all do. They can acknowledge that many of the gains of professional-class working women have been leveraged on the backs of poor women. They can legitimize those women's work and compensate it fairly, which means—at the very least—paying Social Security taxes on it. They can demand that feminists abandon their current fixation on "work-life balance" and on "ending the mommy wars" and instead devote themselves entirely to the real and heart-rending struggle of poor women and children in this country. And they can stop using the hardships of the poor as justification for their own choices. About this much, at least, there ought to be agreement.

> *"The accusation that U.S. working women exploit these immigrants is misguided and ... factually wrong ..."*

Working Mothers Are Not Exploiting Hired Care Givers

Cynthia Fuchs Epstein

Cynthia Fuchs Epstein is a distinguished graduate professor at City University of New York. In the following viewpoint, she argues that despite the claims of recent writers, professional-class women are not exploiting their nannies. In fact, she asserts, very few U.S. nannies are immigrants, and those who are find the work that they do in American homes to be far better than the work they can typically find in their homelands. Epstein writes that making such false accusations against middle-class working women only adds to the challenges they face in the workplace and in society.

As you read, consider the following questions:

1. What percentage of child care in the United States is done by nannies?

2. How many New York City garment workers are immigrants?

3. What fraction of Philippine migrant workers are
   women?

A merican mothers are under attack again. The new attack
is not like that of the 1950s and 1960s, which faulted
stay-at-home mothers for "smother love," "momism," and
schizophrenogenic behavior that turned their sons psychotic.
It is aimed instead at women who hire other women as household help and child-care surrogates, so that the mothers are
free to pursue demanding professional and managerial careers.
These working moms have been denounced as the new ex-
ploiters. Caitlin Flanagan, for example, writing in the March
2004 *Atlantic*, maintains that middle-class women have moved
from the steno pool to corner offices on the backs of women
who live in "serfdom" as their household helpers. . . .

Immigrant workers who come to the United States in the
hope of improving their lives and those of their families face
severe problems; it is important to locate the sources of these
problems and try to deal with them. But the accusation that
U.S. working women exploit these immigrants is misguided
(and, as I will show, factually wrong). Moreover, it reflects or
endorses a cultural bias against middle-class women's entering
the professional and managerial workplace—and a bias also
for what [sociologist] Sharon Hays has identified as "intensive
mothering." Attacks on working mothers are an aspect of a
cultural control system designed to keep women in "their
place," which means, out of the centers of authority and decision making in the society. And the leftists who chastise
women for employing household help unwittingly reinforce
this system. The success of the attacks and chastisements may
be measured in part by the movement of well-trained women
out of top jobs, although not out of the workforce. For example, according to a report by Catalyst, an organization that
monitors women's progress in high level positions, one in
three women MBAs are not working full time. *Time* magazine
recently [as of 2004] reported there has been a considerable

brain drain at the top of the female labor force (among women making more than $55,000 a year)—and, of course, women at the top are few to begin with. Women's access to good jobs at the recruitment level has not translated into top jobs; glass ceilings are mostly still in place, limiting women to a fraction of jobs as senior partners in law and accounting firms, as chief executive officers in corporations, or as full professors in elite universities.

Asked why women are getting off the track to top jobs, commentators often answer that this is their "choice." Yet a look at current debates about women's careers in the press, even at the arguments of liberal writers, shows clearly that professionally trained women are subjected to a barrage of attacks undermining their achievement and fostering a sense of guilt—particularly with regard to their choice to work outside the home and be mothers at the same time.

Misleading Assumptions

It is curious that writers concerned with the perils faced by immigrant workers focus on household labor—particularly child care—when only about 3 percent of child care is done by "nannies" in the United States, and only a small percentage of these nannies are immigrants. (Although the terms are becoming interchangeable, nannies usually work for a salary for the same family and often live on the premises. Babysitters are usually hourly employees who may work for different families.) Recent research by sociologists Kathleen Gerson and Jerry Jacobs finds that most child-care workers are U.S.-born; immigrants make up a small minority. To be sure, many immigrant workers are undocumented, so we can't be certain about their number. But the reports on the conditions of their employment are also questionable. Possibly, immigrants face less exploitation in the homes of high-wage professional women than in other workplaces. Anecdotes about enslaved nannies, whose passports have been taken, are often descriptions of servants employed by wealthy foreigners who bring them from their own countries (and who rarely permit the lady of the household to work in the paid labor force). In any case, we don't have any data on this. . . .

Because most writers who object to the use of child-care surrogates in the home rely on their own experiences and report on their personal ambivalence about not being full-time moms, I offer another picture, drawing on my observations on Manhattan playgrounds, in dinner party chatter, and also on interviews I have done with women working in top law firms in New York City and San Francisco. For these women, the quest for good child-care workers (their husbands invariably delegate the responsibility to them) means offering handsome enough pay packages to compete with other offers, often with benefits and paid vacations, access to cars, and payment for courses to improve the caretakers' skills or language abilities. These working women see it as in their interest to treat nannies well, and, of course, it is.

I don't suggest that home-child-care workers are always well paid, and it is certainly true that a good proportion do not have safety nets. But how do their situations compare with the other opportunities open to them? The writers bemoaning their condition may have stopped eating grapes when Cesar Chavez organized the United Farm Workers' boycott two decades ago, but today [2004] they no doubt eat fruit and vegetables picked by workers in Mexico or Nicaragua, or by migrant families in the United States. I'm sure they wear clothing sewn by women working in factories along the Mexican-U.S. border, far from their homes, subject to dangerous conditions. If these social critics hold conventional jobs (many are freelance writers working at home), they are probably sitting in offices cleaned by unseen janitorsmen and women—toiling at night. They and their husbands or partners and kids play games or watch games played with balls made by third world factory workers; they wear sneakers made by those same workers. At home, their carpets may be made by Pakistani or Indian children. The computers on which they write their attacks are probably assembled by women workers. Nor are these critics suggesting that we stop eating fruit or buying basketballs and computers; they don't mean to raise their own food or return to the yellow pad and pencil. It might just be the case that for many working-class women—immigrant or native—taking care of children in a working couple's middle-class home is preferable to working in a meatpacking plant or cleaning multiple homes in the assembly line process Barbara Ehrenreich described so vividly in her book *Nickel and Dimed*, or working in sweatshops sewing a thousand zippers on blue jeans every working day. (In New York City alone, sixty thousand immigrant workers are employed in the garment industry).

Most female care workers who come from other countries do so with the expectation of improving their lives and the lives of the families their wages help support. Although they face exploitation in the homes of some families, who pay them unfairly and deprive them of the benefits they should have, a good number regard their jobs as attractive, given the limitations they face in the job market because of lack of skills. In time, some of those workers get an education, and as their language skills improve, they go on to work in other sectors. Some women come to the United States to join a husband who has immigrated before them or they are working to bring their husbands here. They send money home for their children or they save money in order to bring their children here at a later date. The jobs open to them outside the home are all at the bottom of the economic ladder.

In their own countries, employment opportunities are often nonexistent. In the Philippines, for example, labor migration is encouraged by the federal government and according to sociologist Gina Mission, some 34 percent to 54 percent of the Filipino population is sustained by remittances from mi-

Nanny Benefits

According to data collected by the International Nanny Association, in 2006 nannies work in the United States received the following benefits:

- 72% of all nannies are paid their normal salary if their employer gives them the day off
- 57% of all nannies receive paid national and religious holidays
- 55% of all nannies receive paid sick days
- 32% of all nannies receive 2 weeks paid vacation
- 32% of all nannies receive use of an employer furnished vehicle
- 29% of all nannies receive paid personal days
- 27% of all nannies receive full reimbursement for use of their own vehicle
- 23% of all nannies receive 1 week paid vacation of their choice
- 20% of all nannies receive 100% employer paid health insurance
- 11% of all nannies receive a paid membership to a spa, gym, country club or health club
- 10% of all nannies receive 50% employer paid health insurance
- 7% of all nannies receive 3 weeks paid vacation
- 5% of all nannies receive 4 weeks paid vacation

International Nanny Association,
"2006 Salary and Benefits Survey Recap," www.nanny.org, 2006.

grant workers, two-thirds of whom are women. Many women also face brutal exploitation in their families in third world countries, where patriarchy dominates and household labor is treated harshly. We have all read articles about women who choose suicide over the slavery imposed in some traditional families. Perhaps these cases do not represent the employment pool from which American families draw their household workers. In any case, when women workers in any society are paid independently, not through the males in their families, they acquire power they never had in the patriarchal systems from which they escaped.

Accusations Against Working Moms

In the "old days"—the bad old days—American women usually lost their jobs when they married and certainly when they had children. It didn't matter that they needed the work or that not having an income meant they had little independence and power in the home. The 1950s model of Mom at home with her kids in a tract house represented a unique moment in history; in all known societies women have worked inside and outside the home at economically productive labor. Responsible for child care in their families, they have had to seek help from their own mothers, sisters, and most often their older children. Under such conditions, exploitation and subjugation were and are common. The women's movement caught fire because women tied to the home, and women already in the workforce but employed in low-level occupations, wanted and needed to move up in the occupational structure. They were able to build on their accumulating legal rights and subsequent developing educational and workplace opportunities. Burdened with child care, but without the supportive kin structure or community life of other societies, they could only find independent solutions to integrating work and home responsibilities. There was no response or support from government, and the market provided few and insufficient resources for child care: unregulated neighborhood caretakers and some commercial centers. In other areas, the market did better. Fast food, twenty-four-hour supermarkets, and even synthetic fabrics were responses to what became the norm—dual-earner families. Within a decade the slow-baked casserole and the homemade layer cake disappeared along with the starched party dress, and no one seemed to miss them. But the old forms of child care are missed (and mythologized)—hence the contemporary debate.

Slowly, a small percentage of women got really good jobs. That meant they had to be "on" at work, more like the men in their lives. And although they faced residual sexism, harassment, and blocked promotions, they were managing to climb ladders once absolutely denied to them. Without wives at home like many of their co-workers, and without the support and admiration of their communities, women had to do more with fewer resources than men. They were begrudged adequate staffs at work (many women secretaries still prefer working for men), and adequate help in their homes. And now they are accused of being oppressors.

They are also accused of failing their children. On the job, they face the same escalation of work hours that men do, and they also must deal with another escalation—of child-care norms that require even more obsessive "hands-on" mothering than in the child-centered Spockian 1950s. Studies of time use at the Urban Institute and elsewhere find that mothers are spending more hours with their children, not less, than in the past. Somehow they find the time, sacrificing their own leisure hours or losing sleep. Yet they are caught in a no-win situation, where they are deemed to be inadequate mothers if they work and inadequate workers if they limit their hours at work.

Our society's romance with child-care perfectionism, its absurd focus on producing "designer children," not only creates pressure on working mothers to reduce their hours in the paid labor force and downscale their hopes for achievement, but may also have poor effects on their children. We don't know yet, but the professionalization of mothering to include constant attention and involvement (from Mozart in the womb to attendance at every sports event and the review of every homework assignment) may not even produce the desired high-quality children. Indeed, it may produce cohorts of narcissistic young people who demand constant attention and never develop the skills of independence. As for the "harm" done to children not cared for by their biological mothers, current research reported in academic circles (but not in the news magazines) by Kathleen Gerson, Ellen Galinsky, and Rosalind Barnett—to name a few—shows no correlation between mothers' working and a variety of psychological problems. And the notion that child care cannot and should not be shared by other women (or men) with less education than the children's mothers is an insult to decent working-class women who have much to offer in the way of compassion, nurturance, and instruction.

Women moving to the top of their work worlds are bombarded with critical messages condemning them for not putting motherhood first. Why shouldn't they have a genuine option, as the men in their lives do, to delegate household and child care and plunge themselves into their work? If this means that their children will be cared for in their homes by surrogates for a period of time, why isn't that a plausible option? The upper classes in many countries follow this pattern, and their children do about as well or poorly as ours do. And many working mothers are quite creative in connecting with their children in profound and meaningful ways (even if these are not to the taste of their critics). The preference for full-time or near full-time mothering undermines the options of our most educated women—and also makes working-class mothers who must work feel that they are failing their children. On the right, this preference serves an ideological position; it keeps women "in their place." On the left, it conveys a message that ambitious women internalize a "male model" of greed and insensitivity at some cost to children and society.

Rightists exhibit a general distaste for women in leadership positions; leftists exhibit the same distaste for women leaders in this (individualist, materialist) society.

Addressing Care—Work

I agree that many families face an excess of time pressures in the modern 24/7 economy and that the workplace generally is not flexible enough in considering the needs of dual-worker families. Too many families do not have enough work to support them in a comfortable lifestyle. For example, single mothers at all income levels, who have no choice about working, lag behind married mothers in their hours of full-time year-round employment. It is difficult for all working families to rear their children in a society that does not support them with publicly provided or subsidized preschool and after-school programs. The solutions that individual families find to these difficulties fall short of the ideals set by the culture. Indeed, the solutions are regarded as another set of problems. Again, wage-earning women are in a no-win situation. So are the women who work for them. Just as we have no meaningful collective policies for providing child care or elder care, so we have no effective policies for enforcing minimum wages, decent benefits, and limited work hours. We do not address care-work as a social priority. Further, the society is generally resistant to unionization. No doubt, it would be difficult to organize household workers, but the effort should be made; ideally, they should be brought into the fold.

It is not helpful, useful, or progressive for a cadre of sisters to suggest that we should discourage individuals from employing the household labor they need to meet the demands of their careers or to suggest that household workers should return to their own homes in the third world, or that American women should do all their housework and child care themselves. Men's obligations are barely on the table, and in all likelihood their participation can't be the solution. Many of them face pressures at work that prevent them from being household and child-care partners, no matter what their ideology.

So, let the name-calling stop and the constructive collective responses begin.

"As these women look up at the 'top,'
they are increasingly deciding that they
don't want to do what it takes to get
there."

Women are Opting Out of the Workplace to Be Stay-at-Home Moms

Lisa Belkin

In the following viewpoint, Lisa Belkin, author of Life's Work:
Confessions of an Unbalanced Mom, *argues that an increasing
number of women are choosing, or opting out, to stay home
from work to take care of their children. She asserts that women
are making this choice because they do not want to hold positions of power, which often bring on great stress and time spent
away from family. Belkin concludes that because women are
willing to leave the workplace to care for their children, corporations will have to work harder at balancing their employees'
work and life responsibilities.*

As you read, consider the following questions:

1. What percentage of the 2003 Yale undergraduate
   class was female?

2. How many of the 108 women who have appeared on *Fortune* magazine's top 50 most powerful women list have chosen to leave their top-level jobs for less demanding pursuits?

3. By what percentage has the number of married men working as full-time caregivers for their children increased?

Wander into any Starbucks in any Starbucks kind of neighborhood in the hours after the commuters are gone. See all those mothers drinking coffee and watching over toddlers at play? If you look past the Lycra gym clothes and the Internet-access cellphones, the scene could be the 50's, but for the fact that the coffee is more expensive and the mothers have M.B.A.'s.

We've gotten so used to the sight that we've lost track of the fact that this was not the way it was supposed to be. Women—specifically, educated professional women—were supposed to achieve like men. Once the barriers came down, once the playing field was leveled, they were supposed to march toward the future and take rightful ownership of the universe, or at the very least, ownership of their half. The women's movement was largely about grabbing a fair share of power—making equal money, standing at the helm in the macho realms of business and government and law. It was about running the world. . . .

Times Have Changed

Arguably, the barriers of 40 years ago are down. Fifty percent of the undergraduate class of 2003 at Yale was female; this year's graduating class at Berkeley Law School was 63 percent women; Harvard was 46 percent; Columbia was 51. Nearly 47 percent of medical students are women, as are 50 percent of undergraduate business majors (though, interestingly, about

30 percent of M.B.A. candidates). They are recruited by top firms in all fields. They start strong out of the gate.

And then, suddenly, they stop. Despite all those women graduating from law school, they comprise only 16 percent of partners in law firms. Although men and women enter corporate training programs in equal numbers, just 16 percent of corporate officers are women, and only eight companies in the *Fortune* 500 have female C.E.O.'s. Of 435 members of the House of Representatives, 62 are women; there are 14 women in the 100-member Senate.

Measured against the way things once were, this is certainly progress. But measured against the way things were expected to be, this is a revolution stalled. During the 90's, the talk was about the glass ceiling, about women who were turned away at the threshold of power simply because they were women. The talk of this new decade is less about the obstacles faced by women than it is about the obstacles faced by mothers. As Joan C. Williams, director of the Program on WorkLife Law at American University, wrote in the *Harvard Women's Law Journal* last spring, "Many women never get near" that glass ceiling, because "they are stopped long before by the maternal wall."

Look, for example, at the Stanford class of '81. Fifty-seven percent of mothers in that class spent at least a year at home caring for their infant children in the first decade after graduation. One out of four have stayed home three or more years. Look at Harvard Business School. A survey of women from the classes of 1981, 1985 and 1991 found that only 38 percent were working full time. Look at professional women in surveys across the board. Between one-quarter and one-third are out of the workforce, depending on the study and the profession. Look at the United States Census, which shows that the number of children being cared for by stay-at-home moms has increased nearly 13 percent in less than a decade. At the same time, the percentage of new mothers who go back to work fell from 59 percent in 1998 to 55 percent in 2000.

Look, too, at the mothers who have not left completely but have scaled down or redefined their roles in the crucial career-building years (25 to 44). Two-thirds of those mothers work fewer than 40 hours a week—in other words, part time. Only 5 percent work 50 or more hours weekly. Women leave the workplace to strike out on their own at equally telling rates; the number of businesses owned or co-owned by women jumped 11 percent since 1997, nearly twice the rate of businesses in general.

Look at how all these numbers compare with those of men. Of white men with M.B.A.'s, 95 percent are working full time, but for white women with M.B.A.'s, that number drops to 67 percent. (Interestingly, the numbers for African-American women are closer to those for white men than to those for white women.). . .

Women Are Rejecting the Workplace

It's not just that the workplace has failed women. It is also that women are rejecting the workplace.

I say this with the full understanding that there are ambitious, achieving women out there who are the emotional and professional equals of any man, and that there are also women who stayed the course, climbed the work ladder without pause and were thwarted by lingering double standards and chauvinism. I also say this knowing that to suggest that women work differently than men—that they leave more easily and find other parts of life more fulfilling—is a dangerous and loaded statement.

And lastly, I am very aware that, for the moment, this is true mostly of elite, successful women who can afford real choice—who have partners with substantial salaries and health insurance—making it easy to dismiss them as exceptions. To that I would argue that these are the very women who were supposed to be the professional equals of men right now, so the fact that so many are choosing otherwise is explosive.

As these women look up at the "top," they are increasingly deciding that they don't want to do what it takes to get there. Women today have the equal right to make the same bargain that men have made for centuries—to take time from their family in pursuit of success. Instead, women are redefining success. And in doing so, they are redefining work.

Time was when a woman's definition of success was said to be her apple-pie recipe. Or her husband's promotion. Or her well-turned-out children. Next, being successful required becoming a man. Remember those awful padded-shoulder suits and floppy ties? Success was about the male definition of money and power.

There is nothing wrong with money or power. But they come at a high price. And lately when women talk about success they use words like satisfaction, balance and sanity.

That's why a recent survey by the research firm Catalyst found that 26 percent of women at the cusp of the most senior levels of management don't want the promotion. And it's why *Fortune* magazine found that of the 108 women who have appeared on its list of the top 50 most powerful women over the years, at least 20 have chosen to leave their high-powered jobs, most voluntarily, for lives that are less intense and more fulfilling.

It's why President Bush's adviser Karen Hughes left the White House, saying her family was homesick and wanted to go back to Austin. It's why Brenda C. Barnes, who was the president and C.E.O. of Pepsi-Cola North America, left that job to move back to Illinois with her family. And it's why Wendy Chamberlin, who was ambassador to Pakistan, resigned, because security concerns meant she never saw her two young daughters.

Why don't women run the world?

Maybe it's because they don't want to. . . .

Opting Out and the Freedom to Choose

Most young women today, having grown up with the assumption of equality, are largely free from guilt about letting feminism down if they leave the fast track. This is probably one reason more women are putting family before career.

Another factor may be that for the younger generation, flexibility is normal. The old, linear "male" model of corporate success—defined as a steady climb from an entry-level position to the highest status one reaches before retirement—has changed, and not just for women. In its place, there is a rich variety of paths that include self-employment, entrepreneurship, and midlife career changes. Women who move in and out of the workforce, or find creative ways to balance work and child rearing, are very much a part of this larger revolution.

The "unfinished revolution" in family roles poses its share of problems. The equilibrium it creates between the sexes is an uneasy one. Currently [as of 2004], women have more freedom than men in choosing whether and how much to work, but they also bear the burden of grappling with those decisions. The "mommy wars" are likely to persist as well: It's difficult to vindicate stay-at-home motherhood without suggesting that working mothers are neglecting their children, or to vindicate working mothers without making stay-at-home mothers feel that their role is not essential.

Still, flexibility and freedom are vastly better than the alternatives. By and large, for the new generation of parents, rigid division of gender roles is obsolete—and so is the stark dichotomy of Superwoman vs. Supermom. That's a good start.

Cathy Young, "Opting Out," Reason Online,
www.reason.com, June 2004.

Biological Imperatives

Any parent can tell you that children are hard-wired from birth: this one is shy, this one is outgoing; this one is laid-back; this one is intense. They were born that way. And any student of the animal kingdom will tell you that males and females of a species act differently. Male baboons leave their mothers; female baboons stay close for life. The female kangaroo is oblivious to her young; the male seahorse carries fertilized eggs to term. Susan Allport, a naturalist, writes in her book *A Natural History of Parenting*, "Males provide direct childcare in less than 5 percent of mammalian species, but in over 90 percent of bird species both male and female tend to their young."

In other words, we accept that humans are born with certain traits, and we accept that other species have innate differences between the sexes. What we are loath to do is extend that acceptance to humans. Partly that's because absolute scientific evidence one way or the other is impossible to collect. But mostly it is because so much of recent history (the civil rights movement, the women's movement) is an attempt to prove that biology is not destiny. To suggest otherwise is to resurrect an argument that can be—and has been—dangerously misused.

"I am so conflicted on this," says Sarah Blaffer Hrdy, an anthropologist and author of *Mother Nature: History of Mothers, Infants and Natural Selection*. Female primates, she says, are "competitive" in that they seek status within their social order. So it would follow that women strive for status too.

But there is an important qualifier. When primates compete, they do so in ways that increase the survival chances of their offspring. In other words, they do it for their children. "At this moment in Western civilization," Hrdy says, "seeking clout in a male world does not correlate with child well-being. Today, striving for status usually means leaving your children with an au pair who's just there for a year, or in inadequate day care. So it's not that women aren't competitive; it's just that they don't want to compete along the lines that are not compatible with their other goals.

"I'm very interested in my family and my environment and my work, not in forging ahead and climbing a power structure," Hrdy explains by way of personal illustration. "That is one of the inherent differences between the sexes." Then she warns, "But to turn that into dogma—women are caring, men are not, or men should have power, women should not, that's dangerous and false.". . .

Temporary Leaves

Talk to any professional woman who made this choice, and this is what she will say. She is not her mother or her grandmother. She has made a temporary decision for just a few years, not a permanent decision for the rest of her life. She has not lost her skills, just put them on hold. . . .

But is it enough insurance? Not only in the event that she needs to go back to work, but also when the time comes, that she wants to. Because at the moment, it is unclear what women like these will be able to go back to. This is the hot button of the work-life debate at the moment, a question on which the future of women and work might well hinge. For all the change happening in the office, the challenge of returning workers—those who opted out completely, and those who ratcheted back—is barely even starting to be addressed.

If that workplace can reabsorb those who left into a career they find fulfilling, then stepping out may in fact be the answer to the frustrations of this generation. If not, then their ability to balance life and work will be no different than their mothers', after all.

On the one hand, there are examples out there of successful women whose careers were not linear. Shirley Tilghman, president of Princeton and the first woman to run the university, spent years deflecting administrative jobs—exactly the sort of jobs that traditionally lead to becoming university president. And Ann Fudge, now chairman and C.E.O. of Young & Rubicam, left the fast track for two years to travel the world with her husband and help start a tutoring program for African-American children.

There are also trends working in these women's favor. One legacy of the dot-com era is that nonlinear career tracks are more accepted and employers are less put off by a resume with gaps and zigzags. Second, a labor shortage is looming in the coming decade, just as this cohort of women may well be planning to re-enter the work force.

"Hidden Brain Drain"

On the other hand, the current economy is hardly welcoming to re-entrants, and the traditional workplace structure does not include a Welcome Back mat. "As a society we have become very good at building offramps," says Sylvia Ann Hewlett, who caused a stir last year [2002] with her book, "Creating a Life," which postulated that the more successful the woman the less likely she was to marry or have children. "But we are seriously lacking onramps."

Hewlett has recently founded the Center for Work-Life Policy and, along with Cornel West, a Princeton professor, and Carolyn Buck Luce, a senior partner at Ernst & Young, has created a task force to study what she calls the "hidden brain drain" of women and minorities from the work force. (I have been invited to join that group.) Task-force members include representatives from a wide range of power bases—large law firms, accounting firms, investment banks and universities— who are coming to recognize that it is not enough to promote and retain talent. You have to acknowledge that talented workers will leave, and you have to find a way to help them come back.

The task force begins its work this winter [2003]. But Hewlett's preliminary research makes her pessimistic about what today's women will face when they want to return to work. At any given time, she says, "two-thirds of all women who quit their career to raise children" are "seeking to re-enter professional life and finding it exceedingly difficult. These women may think they can get back in," she said, when I told her of what I had been hearing in San Francisco and Atlanta and on my own suburban street, where half the women with children at home are not working and where the jobs they quit include law partner and investment banker. "But my data show that it's harder than they anticipate. Are they going to live to the age of 83 and realize that they opted out of a career?" . . .

Women Willing to Leave

This, I would argue, is why the workplace needs women. Not just because they are 50 percent of the talent pool, but for the very fact that they are more willing to leave than men. That, in turn, makes employers work harder to keep them. It is why the accounting firm Deloitte & Touche has more than doubled the number of employees on flexible work schedules over the past decade and more than quintupled the number of female partners and directors (to 567, from 97) in the same period. It is why IBM employees can request up to 156 weeks of job-protected family time off. It is why Hamot Medical Center in Erie, Pa., hired a husband and wife to fill one neonatology job, with a shared salary and shared health insurance, then let them decide who stays home and who comes to the hospital on any given day. It is why, everywhere you look, workers are doing their work in untraditional ways.

Women started this conversation about life and work—a conversation that is slowly coming to include men. Sanity, balance and a new definition of success, it seems, just might be contagious. And instead of women being forced to act like men, men are being freed to act like women. Because women are willing to leave, men are more willing to leave, too—the number of married men who are full-time caregivers to their children has increased 18 percent [as of 2003]. Because women are willing to leave, 46 percent of the employees taking parental leave at Ernst & Young last year were men.

Looked at that way, this is not the failure of a revolution, but the start of a new one. It is about a door opened but a crack by women that could usher in a new environment for us all.

"The lack of women at the top has much more to do with subtle, but tenacious, biases about women and leadership."

Women Are Not Opting Out of the Workplace to Be Stay-at-Home Moms

Deborah Merrill-Sands, Jill Kickul, and Cynthia Ingols

Deborah Merrill-Sands, Jill Kickil, and Cynthia Ingols are professors at the Simmons School of Management in Boston, Massachusetts. In the following viewpoint, they reveal the findings of their 2003–2004 study about professional women's attitudes about leadership and power. According to their data, women are not opting out of the workplace to care for their children. In fact, working mothers want power and leadership just as much as working women without children. The real reason women are leaving the workplace or not moving into high-ranking positions is because of gender discrimination that still permeates the workplace.

Deborah Merrill-Sands, Jill Kickul, and Cynthia Ingols, "Women Pursuing Leadership and Power: Challenging the Myth of the 'Opt Out Revolution,'" *CGO Insights*, February 2005. Reproduced by permission.

As you read, consider the following questions:

1. According to the authors, why are false assertions about women opting out of the workplace disturbing and dangerous?
2. According to the survey, how do women acquire power?
3. According to the survey, what are women's primary goals for exercising power?

Recent media articles have heralded the "Opt Out Revolution," claiming that women are shunning leadership and power at work for full-time motherhood. This claim has garnered remarkable currency. Stories in *The NY Times Magazine, Time, BusinessWeek, Fortune, Fast Company*, and CBS's "60 Minutes" built on one another to create a tenacious narrative that women are choosing to leave or avoid high powered positions at work in order to become full-time parents. Underpinning these arguments is the assertion that women are ambivalent about leadership and power and are willing to sacrifice these to invest in their families.

Patricia Sellers' lead article in *Fortune*'s October 2003 issue on the 50 most powerful women in business was entitled "Power: Do women really want it?" She concluded that women lack power in business largely because they do not want it enough. Lisa Belkin's article in *The New York Times Magazine* led with the title "Q: Why don't more women get to the top? A: They choose not to." Belkin argued that women are not in top leadership roles because they choose to leave the workplace for motherhood. Linda Tischler's February 2004 article, "Where are the women?" in *Fast Company* argued that there are few women in the corner offices in Corporate America because women do not have the drive to compete as hard as men for leadership and power. And in March 2004, *Times* ran a cover story with the headline "The case for staying home: Why more young moms are opting out of the rat race." This article featured women who are "sticking with the kids" rather than staying in the workplace.

Women Are Not "Opting Out"

These assertions about women "opting out" are disturbing and, indeed, dangerous. First, they are stories of a few women. They are based on anecdotal information from small samples of women—primarily privileged, white, female managers and executives—rather than on statistical survey data of large numbers of women. Second, if taken into mainstream thinking, these assertions will curtail opportunities for women. They reinforce gender stereotypes that women are not as committed as men to the world of work and that women do not "have what it takes" to be leaders. And, third, these assertions take the mantle of responsibility for change away from organizations and policymakers and place it squarely on the shoulders of individual women.

Disturbed by the extent to which the notion of the "Opt Out Revolution" has been taken up as "truth" despite little supporting data, the Simmons School of Management collaborated with Hewlett Packard to survey professional women about their views of power and leadership. Our findings challenge the assumptions underlying the purported "Opt Out Revolution." Indeed, women responding to our surveys are pursuing, not shunning, power and leadership. Even more important, they are pursuing leadership and power for goals much broader than their own personal gain and career advancement. They are seeking to strengthen their organizations and make constructive contributions to their communities and society. They are also redefining traditional models of leadership and power, moving from individualistic and hierarchical models of power *over* others to more collaborative models of inclusion and expanding power *through* others. Learning from these women's perspectives can not only help us understand women's career motivations and aspirations, but it can also deepen our understanding of the exercise of power and leadership in the service of building effective organizations.

In 2003 and 2004 we administered two separate, but related, surveys, each to approximately 500 professional and managerial women with extensive work experience attending leadership conferences hosted by the Simmons School of Management. The first survey focused on women's aspirations and views of leadership, while the second focused on women's views of power. Together, the findings from the surveys provide important insights into women's attitudes, aspirations, and use of power and leadership.

Attitudes toward Leadership

Women do aspire to leadership in their organizations. Three-quarters of our respondents indicated that they wanted to be influential leaders in their organizations and viewed this as an important criterion in selecting their next jobs. Importantly, nearly half (47%) aspired to the highest leadership positions.

Interestingly, leadership aspirations do not vary significantly across generations. Indeed, women under 34 had the highest percentage reporting aspirations for leadership influence (78%) and leadership positions (55%). Stories on the "Opt Out Revolution" assert that it is the mid-career women who are exchanging leadership for parenting responsibilities. In contrast, we found no statistically significant difference in the leadership aspirations of women with or without children.

We also found that women of color and white women differed significantly in their aspirations for leadership: 85% of women of color, compared to 70% of white women, aspired to be influential leaders. And 53% of women of color aspired to top leadership positions, compared to 45% of white women. This finding is notable given the paucity of women of color in leadership positions in Corporate America.

Most interesting were women's motivations for pursuing leadership. The majority were not motivated by traditional models of leadership focusing on rank, position, or "turf." Only 28% reported that it was important to them to "be in charge of others." Nor were they primarily motivated by status or rewards. Indeed, only 53% reported that it was important to them to make lots of money. Rather, more than 70% of the women reported that it was important for them to make a difference, help others, contribute to their communities, and make the world a better place

Attitudes toward Power

Women respondents' attitudes toward power echo their attitudes toward leadership. Contrary to conventional wisdom asserting that women are often ambivalent about power, 80% of the 421 women respondents to our 2004 survey on power indicated that they were comfortable with power, respected it, and liked what they could accomplish with it. Similar to our findings on leadership, the majority of women were not pursuing power out of self-interest or for personal gain. Only 45% of the respondents said that they wanted power explicitly to move up the organizational ladder and only 32% indicated that they actively competed for power. In contrast, 65% said that they saw power as important to effective leadership and 70% wanted power in order to change their organizations. Indeed, the most important reason women gave for pursuing power was to make positive contributions to their organizations. Women also drew a clear distinction between exercising power and engaging in "office politics," which they viewed very negatively. Contrary to expectations set by the "Opt Out Revolution" story, we found no significant differences between women with or without children in their attitudes towards power. We also found few generational differences, except that women under 35 had less experience with power and did not agree as strongly as older women that they liked what they could accomplish with power.

To examine power through a gender lens, we asked respondents to characterize their perceptions of the behaviors of powerful men and women in their organizations. Interesting gender differences emerged. While powerful men and women were both seen as "able to make things happen" and "achieve results," men were seen as more likely to assert control *over* others while women were seen as working *with* others to achieve results. There was a significant difference in the extent to which powerful women, as compared to powerful men, were seen to work well with others, make decisions collaboratively, communicate in a compelling manner, and develop others. These findings suggest that women tend to interpret and enact power differently from men. As a group, women are much less comfortable with traditional models of power over others but, indeed, are comfortable in exercising power with and through others.

Women's reliance on exercising power through others, as opposed to over others, is evident in the strategies they use to acquire power. Our statistical modeling revealed that women acquire power by:

- *building relationships*—focusing on empowering their teams or units, supporting co-workers and subordinates, and building networks of allies; and

- *achieving results*—identifying new opportunities, taking risks, and expanding access to resources.

However, even more importantly, our modeling also showed that the most important means our respondents use to acquire power is through first building relationships and then using them to achieve results. Interestingly, the least important strategies for acquiring power are traditional strategies such as developing positional power through direct competition for plum assignments; expanding "turf" or the number of direct reports; working long hours; exchanging favors; and connecting with other powerful people.

More Mothers Are Working Outside the Home

Mothers have always been less likely to work full-time than men or childless women. But that trend is decreasing, not growing. In 1993, the labor force participation of mothers aged 25 to 54 was 14 percent lower than that of childless women in the same age group. By 2000 it was 10 percent lower. By 2004 it was just 8 percent lower. And when women do leave work to take care of their children, most of them return to work sooner than did mothers in generations past. . . .

In the middle layers of income distribution, most wives and mothers are in the labor force most of the time they are raising children. Some experiment with part-time work while their children are young; others stop working for a few years.

But even these women are seldom choosing to opt out. They are shut out by the most backward work-family policies in the industrial world. An international survey by the Council on Contemporary Families found that, of the world's leading industrial countries, only the United States and Australia do not offer government-mandated paid maternity leave. But Australia offers a year of unpaid leave, while the US Family Leave Act guarantees a maximum of just 12 weeks. And half of American workers are not even entitled to that, because they work for companies too small to be covered by the act.

Stephanie Coontz, "Myth of the Opt-Out Mom,"
Christian Science Monitor, *www.csmonitor.com, March 30, 2006.*

We found no significant differences between women with and without children in the ways they acquire and exercise power. However, we did find discernable generational differences. Compared to older women, women under 35 relied equally on results but less on relationships to acquire power.

One of our most striking findings is that women's goals for exercising power, like their goals for leadership, are focused externally on changing their organizations and society more broadly. Our statistical modeling revealed that women's primary goals were 1) *strategic* in that they want to chart the direction of and influence the priorities in their organizations, including ensuring that diversity goals are set and met; and 2) *socially minded* in that they want to ensure that their organizations fulfilled their responsibilities to their communities and that their business operations were socially responsible. Again, these goals for exercising power held constant for women with and without children. Women under 35, especially women of color, were the most adamant that they wanted to use their power for socially minded organizational activities.

Overrated Phenomenon

The issue of mothers "opting out" of the workplace has been overplayed in the media. Women responding to our surveys indicate clearly that they are committed to workplace leadership and to exercising power constructively. In contrast to the assertions of the "Opt Out Revolution" that women with children are turning away from leadership and power to become full-time parents, we found no significant differences between women with children and those without in terms of their attitudes toward leadership and power. Indeed, our data tell a contrasting story. A significantly smaller percentage of women with children (24%) compared to women with no children (31%) reported that they "often think about quitting their job." Moreover, women with children reported higher levels of satisfaction with their opportunities to advance in their organizations.

These findings do not imply that women with children do not face challenges in the workplace. They do. A larger percentage of women with children (48%) than women without children (38%) agreed strongly that they have to adjust their styles to advance. Our data suggest that women are making the adjustments necessary to succeed and at the same time are striving to change their organizations to make them both more effective and more equitable for women.

By challenging women's commitment to work and to their organizations, the "Opt Out Revolution" narrative is detrimental to the majority of women—mothers or not—who are offering constructive leadership in their workplaces. Moreover, taking the spotlight off of organizations and focusing solely on women's individual choices threatens to set back the significant progress that many organizations have made in changing their work culture and practices to ensure that women have the same opportunities as men to take up leadership and contribute fully to their organizations. The top echelon of leadership is the remaining frontier for women. We cannot afford to lose momentum in this arena, especially when we consider the positive motivations that guide women's quest for leadership and power.

Women are redefining leadership and power. Our findings suggest that women are not shunning leadership and power, at least not on their terms. They may be turning away from the more traditional trappings of hierarchical leadership and power, as manifested in office politics, turf-building, and "being in charge of" others. But they are engaging actively in pursuing leadership and power with the aim of achieving bottom-line results, supporting their employees, and making change that is beneficial to their organizations, their communities, and society. Moreover, the majority are exercising power and leadership in ways that are inclusive and collaborative, focused on engaging and empowering followers to achieve organizational goals. Their espoused styles of leadership reflect contemporary models for leadership effectiveness and they are exercising power for positive social ends. This is most apparent in our final statistical model where we combined the ways women acquire power with their goals for exercising power. We found significant interrelationships between how women were using power with others to obtain outcomes that benefited not only their organization and organizations' strategies, but also society more broadly.

Benefits to All

Women pursuing leadership and power benefit all inside and outside our organizations. There is no question that we need leaders who work for the good of their organizations and society. Yet women, the majority of whom espouse and enact these values, continue to hold few positions at the top of our organizations. Our research, and that of many others, suggests that the paucity of women at the top has little to do with their lack of interest in leadership and power or their choices to leave the world of work to pursue parenting. Rather, the lack of women at the top has much more to do with subtle, but tenacious, biases about women and leadership that persist, below the surface and often unrecognized, in organizations today. Indeed, the vigor by which the "Opt Out Revolution" gained currency and escaped scrutiny reflects the power of these deeply held gendered assumptions that continue to shape models of leadership and leaders.

Our findings redirect attention to the changes organizations need to continue to make to ensure that they reap the full benefits of having women as responsible and socially minded organizational leaders. The stark message from our surveys is that while women are committed to their organizations and to pursuing leadership, they still do not see an even playing field. While 89% of the women in the 2003 survey considered that opportunities for women's advancement had improved over the past 10 years, only 58% were satisfied with their own opportunities to advance. Moreover, only 30% believed that women and men have an equal chance of advancing to the highest levels.

The implications of these concerns are sobering. Our statistical modeling revealed that dissatisfaction with advancement opportunities was the most critical factor influencing women's considerations of leaving their organizations. Even more worrisome is that this concern is most prominent among women who see themselves as effective leaders. This lack of satisfaction with advancement is directly related to women's perceptions about whether they have opportunities to exercise power and leadership. The lesson for organizations is that constraining possibilities for women to lead will result in the costly loss of talent. The more intangible, and perhaps more significant, cost is the loss of leaders—leaders who are committed to building effective organizations that serve as exemplary corporate citizens.

Periodical Bibliography

The following articles have been selected to supplement the diverse views presented in this chapter.

Amy J.C. Cuddy, Susan T. Fiske, and Peter Glick	"When Professionals Become Mothers, Warmth Doesn't Cut the Ice," *Journal of Social Issues*, December 2004.
Sanjiv Gupta	"Autonomy, Dependence, or Display? The Relationship Between Married Women's Earnings and Housework," *Journal of Marriage & Family*, May 2007.
Pamela Haag	"Managing Mothers and Mothering Managers," *Antioch Review*, Spring 2006.
Sharon Lerner	"The Motherhood Experiment," *New York Times Magazine*, March 4, 2007.
Denene Millner	"Why I Chose to be a Stay-at-Home Mom," *Ebony*, March 2007.
Sue Shellenbarger	"The Sole Breadwinner's Lament: Having Mom at Home Isn't as Great as It Sounds," *Wall Street Journal—Eastern Edition*, October 10, 2003.
Sondra E. Solomon, Esther D. Rothblum, and Kimberly F. Balsam	"Money, Housework, Sex, and Conflict: Same-Sex Couples in Civil Unions, Those not in Civil Unions, and Heterosexual Married Siblings," *Sex Roles*, May 2005.
Rachel Stauffer	"Not All Women Want to 'Have It All,'" *Chronicle of Higher Education*, May 16, 2007.
Peg Tyre, et al.	"She Works, He Doesn't," *Newsweek*, May 12, 2003.
Thomas Vander Ven and Francis T. Cullen	"The Impact of Maternal Employment on Serious Youth Crime: Does the Quality of Working Conditions Matter?" *Crime and Delinquency*, April 2004.
Fredricka Whitfield	"Why I Chose to Work Outside the Home," *Ebony*, March 2007.

For Further Discussion

Chapter 1

1. Udayan Ray and Archana Rai argue that women must take charge of their own finances in order to better prepare for their futures. Given the other viewpoints in this chapter, do you agree? Why or why not?

2. Evelyn Murphy and E.J. Graff argue that women still earn less than men because of sex discrimination, while Kate O'Beirne argues women are paid less than men because of the choices that they make in and out of the workplace. Whose viewpoint do you find most convincing, and why?

3. What evidence does Carrie L. Lukas offer to support her view that privatizing Social Security will benefit women? What evidence does Mary Hull Caballero offer for why such changes will hurt women? How does each viewpoint influence your understanding of the issue?

4. MomsRising argues that women, especially single mothers, will benefit from a rise in the federal minimum wage, while Jane Galt argues that the opposite is true. After reading both viewpoints, which argument is more convincing? Why?

Chapter 2

1. Mark Trumbull argues that the glass ceiling still keeps women from attaining powerful corporate positions. Linda Hirshman argues that the real glass ceiling begins at home with well-educated wives who choose to stay at home instead of going to work. Whose viewpoint do you think is more persuasive? Why?

2. Eliza Strickland argues that mothers are discriminated against in the workplace, while Jim McGaw argues that fathers are discriminated against. Based on the evidence provided in each viewpoint, do mothers or do fathers face the most discrimination in the workplace?

Chapter 3

1. Ruth Rosen argues that working women must fulfill workplace expectations and also take care of children and other family members, which results in a great deal of stress and anxiety. In addition to the suggestions made by Rosen, what else can be done to help working women balance work and life responsibilities?

2. Mothers Movement Online argues that the Family and Medical Leave Act (FMLA) should be expanded, while the National Coalition to Protect Family Leave argues that the FMLA should be better monitored and enforced before any changes are made. Based on these viewpoints, do you think the FMLA should be expanded or not? Explain your answer.

3. What evidence do Suzanne W. Helburn and Barbara Bergman use to argue that the federal government should subsidize child care? What evidence does Gary Becker use to argue that the federal government should not contribute to child-care funding? Based on the evidence provided, whose viewpoint is most convincing to you, and why?

4. Heather Boushey argues that family-friendly policies are necessary because they help working mothers, while Amy Joyce argues that such policies do not help single employees. Based on these viewpoints, how can employers provide policies that will benefit all employees?

Chapter 4

1. What evidence does Michael Noer give for why career women make bad wives? What evidence does Stephanie Coontz offer for why career women make good wives? Whose viewpoint is most convincing? Why?

2. Caitlin Flanagan argues that working mothers in professional careers are exploiting poor, minority women who serve as their child-care workers, while Cynthia Fuchs Epstein argues that nannies are not being exploited by working mothers. Whose argument is more convincing? Why?

3. Lisa Belkin argues that well-educated women are opting out of the workplace to stay home with their children. Debra Merill-Sands, Jill Kickil, and Cynthia Ingols argue that these women are not opting out of their careers and that the much-publicized reports on this issue have been exaggerated. Based on the evidence provided, which viewpoint is more convincing? Why?

Organizations to Contact

The editors have compiled the following list of organizations concerned with the issues debated in this book. The descriptions are derived from materials provided by the organizations. All have publications or information available for interested readers. The list was compiled on the date of publication of the present volume; the information provided here may change. Be aware that many organizations take several weeks or longer to respond to inquiries, so allow as much time as possible.

9to5, National Association of Working Women
207 E Buffalo St., #211, Milwaukee, WI   53202
(414) 274-0925 • fax: (414) 272-2870
e-mail: 9to5@9to5.org
Web site: www.9to5.org

9to5 is a national, grassroots membership organization that strengthens women's ability to work for economic justice in such areas as sexual harassment, work/family challenges, and pay equity. Founded in 1973, 9to5 has a membership of mainly low-wage women, women in traditionally female jobs, and those who've experienced any form of discrimination. In addition to the *9to5 Newsline* newsletter, 9to5 also publishes reports about women and work, including "The 9to5 Guide to Combating Sexual Harassment: Candid Advice from 9to5, National Association of Working Women" and "The Job Family Challenge: Not for Women Only."

American Business Women's Association (ABWA)
9100 Ward Parkway, PO Box 8728
Kansas City, MO   64114-0728
(800) 228-0007 • fax: (816) 361-4991
e-mail: abwa@abwa.org
Web site: www.abwa.org

Founded in 1949, the ABWA brings together businesswomen of diverse occupations and provides opportunities for them to help themselves and others grow personally and professionally through leadership, education, networking support, and national recognition. In addition to hosting a national conference, scholarship competition, and professional development workshops, the ABWA also publishes the bi-monthly magazine, *Women in Business.*

Business and Professional Women/USA (BPW/USA)
1900 M St. NW, Suite 310, Washington, DC   20036
(202) 293-1100 • fax: (202) 861-0298
e-mail: foundation@bpwfoundation.org
Web site: www.bpwusa.org

Founded in 1919, BPW/USA is a multigenerational, nonpartisan membership organization that focuses on issues of working women. One of the first women's organizations to endorse the Equal Rights Amendment, in 1937, BPW/USA has been a successful leader in promoting and supporting legislation affecting working women ever since. In addition to three national conferences, BPW/USA communicates its research and objectives through a bimonthly newsletter and a quarterly journal, *Business Woman.*

Catalyst
120 Wall Street, 5th Floor, New York, NY   10005
(212) 514-7600 • fax: (212) 514-8470
e-mail: info@catalyst.org
Web site: www.catalyst.org

Catalyst is a research and advisory organization working with businesses and the professions to build inclusive environments and expand opportunities for women at work. As an independent, nonprofit membership organization formed in 1962, Catalyst conducts research on all aspects of women's career advancement and provides strategic and web-based consulting services globally. In addition to annual reports, Catalyst has also published many in-depth studies, including "Advancing African-American Women in the Workplace: What Managers Need to Know" and "After-School Worries: Tough on Parents, Bad for Business."

The Christian Working Woman (TCWW)

PO Box 1210, Wheaton, IL   60189
(630) 462-0552 • fax: (630) 462-1613
e-mail: tcww@christianworkingwoman.org
Web site: www.christianworkingwoman.org

TCWW began in 1984 as an outgrowth of a ministry for workplace women that began at The Moody Church in Chicago, Illinois. It is a nonprofit organization aimed at helping working women practice the teachings of Christ in the workplace. As of 2007, TCWW produced two radio program formats, distributed books and materials, and organized retreats and conferences in the United States and abroad. Web site visitors can subscribe to *The Christian Working Woman Newsletter*, a free quarterly publication.

Coalition of Labor Union Women (CLUW)

815 Sixteenth St. NW, 2nd Floor South
Washington, DC   20006
(202) 508-6969 • fax: (202) 508-6968
e-mail: getinfo@cluw.org
Web site: www.cluw.org

Formed in 1974, CLUW is a nonpartisan organization within the union movement whose primary goal is to unify all union women in a viable organization to determine the common problems and concerns of women in the workplace and to develop action programs within the framework of existing unions. At its founding convention in Chicago, Illinois, CLUW adopted four basic goals of action that remained important to its members: to promote affirmative action in the workplace; to strengthen the role of women in unions; to organize the unorganized women; and to increase the involvement of women in the political and legislative process. In addition to regular health factsheets, CLUW publishes informational leaflets and reports, including "Sharing Our Stories: Voices at Work" and "It's Not Funny, It's Not Flattering: Sexual Harassment."

National Association for Female Executives (NAFE)
60 E. Forty-second St., Suite 2700, New York, NY 10165
(800) 927-6233
e-mail: nafe@nafe.com
Web site: www.nafe.com

NAFE is one of the nation's largest women's professional associations and the largest women business owners' association, providing resources and services—through education, networking, and public advocacy—to empower its members to achieve career success and financial security.

National Partnership for Women & Families (NPWF)
1875 Connecticut Ave. NW, Suite 650
Washington, DC 20009
(202) 986-2600 • fax: (202) 986-2539
e-mail: info@nationalpartnership.org
Web site: www.nationalpartnership.org

From outlawing sexual harassment to prohibiting pregnancy discrimination to giving 50 million Americans family and medical leave, the National Partnership for Women & Families has fought for every major policy advancement that has helped women and families since the 1970s. As a vocal advocate on the issues that are most important to women and families, the NPWF presses for family-friendly workplace policies and fights discrimination in all its forms. The NPWF frequently issues reports on a variety of workplace issues, including "Privatizing Social Security Would Harm African American Women," "Why Paid Sick Days Make Good Business Sense," and "The Pregnancy Discrimination Act: 25 Years Later."

Women Employed (WE)
111 N. Wabash, Suite 1300, Chicago, IL 60602
(312) 782-3902 • fax: (312) 782-5249
e-mail: info@womenemployed.org
Web site: www.womenemployed.org

Since 1973, WE has fought to outlaw pay discrimination, pregnancy discrimination, and sexual harassment, and to strengthen federal equal opportunity policies and work/family benefits. It brings people and organizations together to improve women's economic status by expanding employment opportunities for thousands of women each year. In addition to its *Monthly Newsbyte*, WE regularly publishes research reports on the status of working women, including "Raising Women's Pay: An Agenda For Equity" and "Pathways and Progress: Best Practices to Ensure Fair Compensation."

Women Work! The National Network for Women's Employment

1625 K Street, NW, Suite 300, Washington, DC   20006
(800) 235-2732 • fax: (202) 467-5366
e-mail: info@womenwork.org
Web site: www.womenwork.org

Since 1978, the network has assisted more than 10 million women to successfully enter, reenter, and advance in the workforce by advancing economic justice and equality for women through education, advocacy, and organizing. Through supporting, advocating, and advancing women's economic self-sufficiency, Women Work! members strengthen families and communities. In addition to regularly publishing the *eNews* newsletter, Women Work! publishes a weekly bulletin, *Economic Equality Insider*, and a quarterly magazine, *We Work!*

Women Working Worldwide (WWW)

MMU Manton Building, Rosamond St. West
Manchester   M15 6LL
   UK
+44 (0)161 247-6171
e-mail: information@women-ww.org
Web site: www.poptel.org.uk/women-ww

WWW is a United Kingdom-based organization that conducts collaborative research and campaign initiatives with partners in Asia, Central America, Africa, and Eastern Europe. Since its founding in 1985, WWW has focused on supporting the rights of women working in supply chains that supply the UK and other European countries with consumer goods. WWW's recent annual reports include "Core Labour Standards and the Rights of Women Workers in International Supply Chains," "Women Workers and Codes of Conduct," and "Women Workers & Social Causes."

Bibliography of Books

Barbara R. Bergmann — *The Economic Emergence of Women.* 2nd ed. New York: Palgrave Macmillan, 2005.

Francine D. Blau, Marianne A. Ferber, and Anne E. Winkler — *The Economics of Women, Men, and Work.* 6th ed. Upper Saddle River, NJ: Pearson/Prentice Hall, 2006.

Uta Blohm — *Religious Traditions and Personal Stories: Women Working as Priests, Ministers, and Rabbis.* New York: Peter Lang, 2005.

Tito Boeri, Daniela Del Boca, and Christopher Pissarides, eds. — *Women at Work: An Economic Perspective.* New York: Oxford University Press, 2005.

Dorothy Sue Cobble — *The Other Women's Movement: Workplace Justice and Social Rights in Modern America.* Princeton, NJ: Princeton University Press, 2004.

Fiona Colgan and Sue Ledwith, eds. — *Gender, Diversity, and Trade Unions: International Perspectives.* New York: Routledge, 2002.

Susanna Delfino and Michele Gillespie, eds. — *Neither Lady nor Slave: Working Women of the Old South.* Chapel Hill: University of North Carolina Press, 2002.

Marcelle Langan DiFalco and Jocelyn Greenky Herz — *The Big Sister's Guide to the World of Work: The Inside Rules Every Working Girl Must Know.* New York: Simon and Schuster, 2005.

Susan K. Dyer, ed. *Women at Work.* Washington, DC: American Association of University Women Educational Foundation, 2003.

Lisel Erasmus-Kritzinger *Inspirational Women at Work: 52 Personal and Life Experiences Shared to Empower, Encourage, Uplift, and Inspire.* Pretoria, IL: LAPA, 2003.

Jeanie Ahearn Greene *Blue-Collar Women at Work with Men: Negotiating the Hostile Environment.* Westport, CT: Praeger, 2006.

Sharlene Nagy Hesse-Biber and Gregg Lee Carter *Working Women in America: Split Dreams.* New York: Oxford University Press, 2005.

Saul D. Hoffman and Susan L. Averett *Women and the Economy: Family, Work, and Pay.* Boston: Pearson Addison Wesley, 2005.

Alice Kessler-Harris *Gendering Labor History.* Urbana: University of Illinois Press, 2007.

Sharon H. Mastracci *Breaking Out of the Pink-Collar Ghetto: Policy Solutions for Non-College Women.* Armonk, NY: M.E. Sharpe, 2004.

Nan Mooney *I Can't Believe She Did That: Why Women Betray Other Women at Work.* New York: St. Martin's Press, 2005.

Julianne Nelson *Women Working It Out: Career Plans and Business Decisions.* Lanham, MD: University Press of America, 2003.

Deborah Perry
Piscione

The Many Faces of 21st Century Working Women: A Report to the Women's Bureau of the U.S. Department of Labor. McLean, VA: Education Consortium, LLC, Choose 2 Lead Women's Foundation, 2004.

Mary Lou
Quinlan

Time Off for Good Behavior: How Hard Working Women Can Take a Break and Change Their Lives. New York: Broadway Books, 2005.

Kate Raworth

Trading Away Our Rights: Women Working in Global Supply Chains. Oxford, U.K.: Oxfam GB, 2004.

Krista
Scott-Dixon

Doing IT: Women Working in Information Technology. Toronto: Sumach Press, 2004.

Tina Schwager
and Michele
Schuerger

Cool Women, Hot Jobs . . . and How You Can Go for It, Too! Minneapolis, MN: Free Spirit, 2002.

Eugene
Smolensky and
Jennifer Appleton
Gootman, eds.

Working Families and Growing Kids: Caring for Children and Adolescents. Washington, DC: National Academies Press, 2003.

Emilie Stoltzfus

Citizen, Mother, Worker: Debating Public Responsibility for Child Care after the Second World War. Chapel Hill: University of North Carolina Press, 2003.

Sharon Hartman
Strom

Women's Rights. Westport, CT: Greenwood Press, 2003.

Leora Tanenbaum   *Catfight: Women and Competition.*
New York: Seven Stories Press, 2002.

Reg Theriault   *The Unmaking of the American Working Class.* New York: New Press, 2003.

Index

W

Christina Fisanick, ed.

Working women: opposing viewpoints